THE

PRINCIPLE AND THE METHOD

OF THE

HEGELIAN DIALECTIC

A DEFENCE OF THE DIALECTIC
AGAINST ITS CRITICS

BEING A

THESIS ACCEPTED BY THE FACULTY OF THE COLLEGE OF LETTERS
IN THE UNIVERSITY OF CALIFORNIA IN PART FULFILMENT
OF THE REQUIREMENTS FOR THE DEGREE OF
DOCTOR OF PHILOSOPHY

BY

EVANDER BRADLEY McGILVARY

PART I

THE PRINCIPLE OF THE DIALECTIC

Reprinted from the PHILOSOPHICAL REVIEW, Vol. VI, No. 5

BERKELEY
UNIVERSITY OF CALIFORNIA
1897

THE

PRINCIPLE AND THE METHOD

OF THE

HEGELIAN DIALECTIC

A DEFENCE OF THE DIALECTIC
AGAINST ITS CRITICS

BEING A

THESIS ACCEPTED BY THE FACULTY OF THE COLLEGE OF LETTERS
IN THE UNIVERSITY OF CALIFORNIA IN PART FULFILMENT
OF THE REQUIREMENTS FOR THE DEGREE OF
DOCTOR OF PHILOSOPHY

BY

EVANDER BRADLEY McC 'VARY

PART I

THE PRINCIPLE OF THE DIALECTIC

Reprinted from the PHILOSOPHICAL REVIEW, Vol. VI, No. 5

BERKELEY
UNIVERSITY OF CALIFORNIA
1897

PREFACE

———•◦•———

HEGEL'S *Logic* has been the object of attack upon every conceivable ground. Hence no defence of it can be circumstantial without falling under the category of the false Infinite. Wishing to keep out of that category, I have attempted to defend the *Logic* against two objections only; but these are the most vital objections, for it seems to me that the most significant attacks that have been made against the Hegelian dialectic have been attacks upon the very *conception* of that dialectic, or attacks upon the *consistency and uniformity of the method* which the dialectic pursues. Those who repudiate the very conception of the dialectic take as their theme the impossibility of treating logic as an organic science without the aid of experience; for they conceive the Hegelian dialectic as a science apart, and of course they have no very great difficulty in showing the impossibility of such a science. Those who attack the method of the dialectic generally try to convict that method of inconsistency and vacillation. To them it seems to be rather a *lack* of method, a blind fumbling and a grasping of whatever comes within reach if, peradventure, it may serve the purpose in hand.

In accordance with the desire to be brief in my discussion of the subjects undertaken, I have merely attempted, in answer to criticisms of the first class, to show what was really Hegel's claim with regard to the alleged presuppositionless character of the *Logic*, what his view of the relation of logic to experience, and what his justification for beginning the dialectical movement where he begins it. In treating the second class of criticisms, I have taken Mr. McTaggart's treatise as fairly representative of the others. I have done this because it is the most recent work on the subject and is probably fresh in the reader's mind; because it is able and clear; and, above all,

because it brings out into desirable prominence the points at
issue. As against Mr. McTaggart, I have tried to prove that
external reflection is not used in the dialectic movement proper,
and that the negative is the one power that moves the whole
machinery.

In quoting from Hegel I have confined myself almost exclu-
sively to his larger *Science of Logic*, designated in the following pages as the *Greater Logic*. It seems desirable to make
that larger work the basis of this discussion for several reasons:
the dialectical element is much more fully developed and
exhibited in it than in the *Logic* of the *Encyclopaedia ;* it is a
much more unfamiliar work to English readers, and thus may
throw new light on the topics under treatment; it has been
neglected by most of the critics of Hegel, and should be
restored to the position of importance it rightfully occupies in
the Hegelian system; and, lastly and chiefly, it represents
Hegel's ripest views on logic. The first volume, from which
most of my quotations are taken, had been thoroughly revised
just before the author's untimely death. This fact must be
emphasized, for we so often read nowadays that the *Lesser
Logic* is the latest authentic record of the great dialectician's
views of dialectic. One would think, from many representa-
tions in modern works, that the *Greater Logic* was a juvenile
production, definitively shelved when the *Encyclopaedia* appeared on the scene. Fortunately, we have unmistakable testimony of Hegel's own appreciation of the more elaborate
performance, in the fact that he reissued, or, rather, prepared to
reissue, that work in 1831. Unhappily he was cut short in the
midst of that revision ; but not before he had written enough
— the whole first volume — to show what were his latest views
on this the cardinal science in his system. The *Greater Logic* is
so full in its treatment of the principle or presupposition of the
dialectic and in its exposition of the method of that dialectic,
that it hardly leaves anything to be desired — except, perhaps,
the doing of it all into vernacular German or English. All I
undertake to do in these little papers is to bring out clearly by
quotations Hegel's doctrine, and to set this doctrine over
against the misrepresentations that have been too current both

within and without the Hegelian schools. For Hegel as he is written about is not always Hegel as he wrote.

This preface must not be brought to a close without a word of acknowledgment to my esteemed teacher and friend, Dr. George Holmes Howison, Mills Professor of Intellectual and Moral Philosophy and Civil Polity in the University of California. He it was who led me to begin the study of Hegel, and, in my first attempts to catch the spirit and understand the significance of Hegel's philosophy, gave me the benefit of his ripe knowledge. My subsequent study has been carried on in close touch with him, and, although the views expressed in this paper are not coincident in all points with his views, still I owe more than I can estimate to the stimulus and the suggestiveness of his criticisms.

1897.

THE PRESUPPOSITION QUESTION IN HEGEL'S LOGIC.

PERHAPS the objection most often urged against Hegel's logic is that it is not true to its claim of making no presuppositions. Almost every critic of the logic dwells at great length upon the absurdity of such a claim and upon the consequent impossibility of making it good. For instance, Trendelenburg says: "It is the fundamental thought of the Hegelian dialectic, that pure thought, out of its own immanent necessity, without presupposition, begets and knows the moments of Being." Then he goes on to ask: "Is there such a logical beginning without presupposition, a beginning in which thought has nothing but itself, and scorns all imagery and perception, and thus deserves the name of pure thought?"[1] His answer to the question is, "No." For all through Hegel's dialectic there can be detected the presence of perception and, in particular, of spatial motion, as presuppositions of the whole logical movement and as its motive power. It is needless to quote from the other critics. *Ab uno disce omnes.*

An unsuspicious reader of the above extract will take for granted that Hegel really claims that his logic is without any presupposition; and although the passage admits of a double interpretation, still the whole discussion following it is without any meaning unless it is directed against the alleged pretension of a presuppositionless logic. But a careful study of Hegel's logic shows that no such pretension is made. On the contrary, Hegel expressly states that his logic has a presupposition; and he states it so explicitly that the wonder is that so many critics have followed Trendelenburg and ignored Hegel. In the Preface to his *Greater Logic,* in the Introduction, and in the body of that work, in which he devotes a whole chapter to the question, "With what must the Science begin?" Hegel unambiguously says that his *Logic* presup-

[1] *Logische Untersuchungen,* 3d ed., vol. i, pp. 36, 37.

poses the result of the *Phenomenology of the Spirit.* In order that such an assertion may not appear unsupported, I will quote some of the passages that leave the matter no longer in doubt. The passage in the Introduction runs thus: "In the *Phenomenology of the Spirit* I have exhibited consciousness in its progress from the first immediate opposition of itself and its object, on to absolute knowledge. This course traverses all the forms of the relation of consciousness to its object, and has as its result the conception of our science. This conception needs no justification here, — apart from the fact that it comes out as the final result in the *Logic* itself, — it needs no justification here, because it got its justification there " (in the *Phenomenology*). "And it is capable of no other justification than just this production of it by consciousness, all whose own peculiar forms are resolved into this conception as their truth. . . . This conception of the pure science and the deduction of it are presupposed in this present treatise, in so far as the *Phenomenology of the Spirit* is nothing else but such a deduction of it." [1] Again, in his discussion of the question, "With what must the Science begin?" he says: "The beginning is *logical*, in that it should be made in the element of free, independent thought, in pure knowledge. It is *mediated* therefore by the fact that pure knowledge is the last absolute truth of consciousness. It has been remarked in the Introduction that the *Phenomenology of the Spirit* is the science of consciousness, the exhibition of the fact that consciousness has the conception of our science, that is, of pure knowledge, as its result. To this extent, then, the logic has the science of the Phenomenal Spirit as its presupposition ; for that science contains and displays the necessity, and hence the proof of the truth, of the standpoint of pure knowledge, as well as the way in which that standpoint is reached." [2] In two or three sentences he characterizes the starting-point and the movement of the

---

[1] I, 31, 32 (33–35). I use the 1841 issue of the second edition of the *Greater Logic ;* but give the paging of the issue of 1833–4 in parenthesis. It should be remembered that the first volume of the second edition was carefully revised by its author just before his death.

[2] I, 57 (61).

Phenomenology, and then proceeds : " In that treatise, immediate consciousness is also the first and immediate fact in the science ; in the *Logic,* however, that is the presupposition, which had proved to be the result of that former study, viz., the Idea as pure knowledge." [1] Again : " Here Being is the initial category (*das Anfangende*), exhibited as arising by mediation, a mediation that at the same time cancels itself ; and there is present the presupposition of pure knowledge, as the result of finite knowledge or consciousness." [2]

These passages could not be clearer or more decisive as to Hegel's meaning. The presupposition of the *Logic* is the *Phenomenology,* and the presupposition of the *Phenomenology* is immediate, sensuous consciousness. Hegel's thought, then, is this : If sensuous consciousness is an unquestionable point of departure, — and no one can deny that it is, — then it can be shown conclusively that the point of view of absolute knowledge is attainable from this starting-point. And if this point of view of absolute knowledge is a legitimate point of view, then a logic such as he proceeds to develop is a legitimate science ; for the subject-matter of such a science rises objectively before the view of one who reaches that eminence.

We have now arrived at the point where we can see what reply Hegel would make to the charge that concrete experience furnishes him with the motive power for his logical machinery. He would say that Absolute Idealism, and logic as a science in the system of Absolute Idealism, do not pretend to teach that man can think in complete and utter isolation from sensuous experience. If man could and did so think, such thought would not be the pure absolute thought that logic demands; but it would be a falsely infinite, abstract thought, which could not be absolute for the very reason that it has beyond it, and therefore limiting it, an experience in which sense plays a part. The progress in the *Phenomenology* from sensuous consciousness to absolute knowledge does not consist in " shuffling off the mortal coil " of sense, but in making " the mortal put on immortality," — to speak plainly, it con-

---

[1] I, 57, 58 (62).　　　　　[2] I, 58, 59 (63).

sists in showing that the sense element in consciousness is not an independent ingredient that may as well stand outside of knowledge as within it; but that this sense element is, in its very nature, a moment in absolute knowledge, included essentially in absolute knowledge and not in any ultimate opposition to it.

Many passages could be quoted from the *Logic* to show that the thought that logic deals with is not abstract thought in the ordinary sense of the word 'abstract'; it is not an element in experience *merely coördinate* with sense, and furnishing the form to experience while sense furnishes the matter. In a passage in the Preface to the second edition, Hegel discusses the ordinary view taken of the function of thought, and repudiates it. " The indispensable basis, the Conception, the Universal, which is thought itself in so far as we can abstract only from image-presentation (*Vorstellung*) in the wor   con-not be regarded as *only* an indifferent form, v   indif-ferently on a content. But these thoughts   and spiritual things, which thoughts are themse es the s.   ntial content, are such a content as contains . ultiple deur/mina-tions, and has in it also the distinction of a su   nd   body, of conception and a relative reality. The deepei   sis is the true Soul (*die Seele für sich*), the pure Conception, which is the innermost principle of all objects, their simple life-pulse, as well as the life-pulse of subjective thought." [1] This passage is so very important in helping to orient one in Hegel's philosophy, and therefore in Hegel's *Logic*, that it will perhaps be permissible to dwell upon it further. And in order to obtain a better understanding of it, it will be well to contrast the view expressed in it with the view of thought held by Lotze, by Mr. F. H. Bradley, and by almost every one else, and made the basis by Mr. McTaggart [2] for an attempted justification of Hegel. This ordinary view finds expression in such language as this: " Thought is everywhere but a mediating activity moving hither and thither, bringing into connection the original intuitions of external and internal perception, which are

[1] I, 16, 17 (18).   [2] *Studies in the Hegelian Dialectic.*

predetermined by fundamental ideas and laws the origin of
which cannot be shown; it develops special and properly logical forms, peculiar to itself, only in the effort to apply the idea
of truth (which it finds in us) to the scattered multiplicity of
perceptions, and of the consequences developed from them.
Hence nothing seems less justifiable than the assertion that
this Thinking is identical with Being, and that Being can be
resolved into it without leaving any residuum; on the contrary,
everywhere in the flux of thought there remain quite insoluble
those individual nu.. which represent the several aspects of
that important content which we designate by the name of
Being." [1] This view find more trenchant expression in such
sentences as these: "Thought, in its actual processes and
results, cannot transcend the dualism of the ' that ' and the
' what.' " " Truth and thought are not the thing itself, but are
of it and about it." " For I do not deny that reality *is* an
object of thought; I deny that it is barely and *merely* so. If
you rest here on a distinction between thought and its object,
that opens a further question to which I shall return. But if
you admit that in asserting reality to fall within thought, you
meant that in reality there is nothing beyond what is made
thought's object, your position is untenable." [2] These statements form an excellent contrast against which Hegel's doctrine can be easily understood. Thought as only a mediating
activity, thought as *ex*clusive of thing, these two complementary conceptions are emphasized by the logical dualists I have
just quoted. Thought as not merely a mediating activity,
thought as *in*clusive of thing, are the conceptions emphasized

---

[1] Lotze, *Microcosmos*, p. 354 of the second volume of the English translation.
I have quoted the passage Mr. McTaggart quotes, but it could easily be paralleled
by numerous passages from Lotze's *Logic*.

[2] F. H. Bradley's *Appearance and Reality*, pp. 168, 169. See the whole chapter, where, although he admits that this dualism is not absolute and must be
transcended, he maintains that such transcendence is not within the power of
thought. The last sentence quoted above is ambiguous, and it seems to me that
Mr. Bradley makes out the untenability of his opponent's position by taking
advantage of this ambiguity. If by ' what is made thought's object ' is meant
what in time has already been so made, then *cadit quaestio*. If not, the untenability of the adversary's position is not so easily proved.

by Hegel as requisite to the intelligent and truly profitable
reading of his *Logic.* He devotes four pages of his Preface to
the discussion and refutation of the view that thought and
thing stand against each other in a dualistic relation which
thought cannot transcend. Hegel's view of thought can be
summed up in one term, so often misunderstood, but a term
that he has taken much pains to rescue from such a fate.
Hegel's thought is *begreifendes Denken.*[1] We English-speak-
ing people, in borrowing our words 'conceive,' 'concept,'
'conception,' from a dead language, have lost the striking
imagery that could have been called up in a Roman mind by
these words. The Germans are more fortunate in having a
native word, which, though the metaphor in it has faded, still
has cognates that can revive the metaphor. *Begreifendes
Denken* is grasping, clutching thought, thought that grips its
object as its own inalienable possession. Perhaps we might
translate *das begreifende Denken,* by the phrase 'object-appro-
priating thought'; for the logical relation of such thought to
its object is analogous to the legal relation of the master to the
slave; the slave had no independent status; he stood only
in his master, who engulfed him. Hegel also calls thought
objectives Denken, inasmuch as it transcends the distinction
between subject and object. "Pure science, accordingly, presupposes emancipation from the opposition of consciousness.
It contains *thought in so far as it is just as much the object-
matter in itself, or the object-matter in itself in so far as it is
just as much pure thought.* As Science, the truth is the pure
self-developing self-consciousness, and has the form of self, in
that the *absolute is known conception, but the conception as such
is the absolute.* This objective thought, then, is the content
of pure Science."[2] Again, in another place, a few lines lower,
what he says seems to have Mr. Bradley prophetically in mind,
for there we read: "In Logic we do not have to do with
thought *about* something that lies independently outside of
thought and is the basis of that thought."[3] Again, compare
with the passage formerly quoted from Lotze, this passage

[1] I, 25 (27).   [2] I, 33 (35).   [3] I, 33 (36).

from Hegel: "Logic is accordingly determined as the science of pure thought, and has as its principle pure knowledge, the unity which is not abstract but concrete and living, because in it the opposition for consciousness of a subjectively independent being and of a second such being, an object, is known as transcended, and Being of itself is known as pure Conception, and pure Conception as true Being." [1] Once more: "Logic is the *pure Science*, that is, pure knowledge in the whole compass of its development. This idea [of pure knowledge], however, has defined itself in that result [*i.e.*, of the *Phenomenology*] to be certainty become truth, certainty which, on the one hand, no longer stands with its object over against it; it has taken its object into itself, knows its object as its own very self. On the other hand, it has transcended the knowledge of itself as of something that stands over against the objective and is its denial; thought has rid itself of this subjectivity and is a unity with its riddance." [2]

It would not have been necessary, in quoting these passages in justification of my interpretation of Hegel's meaning, to pile Pelion on Ossa, were it not that the most recent critic and defender of Hegel gives it out as probably, if not certainly, Hegel's view, that the 'datum' as he calls it, is not identical with thought.

Having thus shown what Hegel's attitude was towards the relation of thought to its objects, objects of sensuous experience among others, I can now return to the charge which I began to discuss above,[3] the charge that Hegel surreptitiously makes use of sensuous experience and its living, moving reality, in order to get life and movement into his pure thought. According to Hegel's view, such a charge would be preposterous in the literal sense of the word. The living, moving reality of nature has no independence; *it is merely the expression of the life of thought*. It is only in thought that nature "lives and moves and has its being." In the Preface to the first edition, Hegel says: "The development of all natural and spiritual life rests on the nature of the pure essences alone, that constitute the content of Logic."[1]　In another place, he says that the immanent negativity which is the principle of the logical movement is "the principle of all natural and spiritual life."[2]　The question with Hegel, as with Kant, is not whether nature, external or internal, physical or psychical, is one vast system of forces and of life; but the question is *whence* comes that life.　Does it belong to nature as an independent kingdom, or is the kingdom thought's own ?　And as Kant answered this question by recognizing the constitutional sovereignty of thought in the world of sense, by acknowledging a power not nature's self, that works in nature's life, so Hegel answered the same question by recognizing the same sovereignty and the same power — but with a difference: the sovereignty is *absolute*.　Trendelenburg, Haym, and Schmid might thus have spared their pains in showing that Hegel borrowed from experience his motive power, stole from the heaven of sensuous perception the fire to make the earth of his logical categories warm into the semblance of life.　It was incumbent upon them to overthrow the Critical Philosophy in its subordination of the world of experience to logic, before claiming such an easy victory over the Absolute Philosophy.　For the very elements, which, according to the above-named critics, Hegel stole from experience and smuggled into thought, had already been shown by Kant to have been lent to experience by thought.

But the question will be asked : Is, then, Hegel's logic after all not a science of abstract thought ?　Does not Hegel himself define logic as "the science of the pure idea in the abstract element of thought"?　Two answers can be given to these questions, varying according to what is meant by 'abstract' and by 'pure.'　If by 'abstract thought' and 'pure thought' is meant thought thinking away with nothing to think, somewhat like Browning's "roses embowering with naught they embower," there is one answer, a categorical "No."　But if by abstraction is meant *abstraction from the abstraction* of ordinary consciousness which sets sense over

[1] I, 7 (7, 8).　　　　　[2] I, 41.

against thought, *abstraction from sense as an absolute other to thought*, then there is another answer: "Logic *is* abstract." And if by 'pure' is meant refined from the common-sense error that thought must mix itself with an external matter before it can do execution upon it, then logical thought is pure. In saying all this I am not resorting to subtleties of rhetoric to avoid surrendering to the exigencies of inevitable exegesis. I am merely reading Hegel's definition of logic in the *Encyclopaedia* in the light of a prolonged explanation of its subject-matter in the *Greater Logic* which some, who glibly quote the *Encyclopaedia*, have not done him the honor to read and study.

If the reader will open the *Greater Logic* on page 58 (62), he will find these words: "Pure knowledge, *as having consolidated into this unity* [of the subjective and the objective] has sublated all reference to another and to mediation; it is the distinctionless." This is the way in which logic comes by its abstract character; it is not by refusing to transcend the distinction between thought and its object and thus maintaining itself in the sphere of the very *different* abstraction of finite consciousness; but it is by transcending that distinction.

But along with this transcending of the distinction that belongs to ordinary consciousness, there comes another feature that to ordinary consciousness appears as an abstraction, namely, the failure to notice the sensuous nature of the object, in so far as it is *merely* sensuous. Of course, in so far as the nature of an object is merely sensuous, it is abstract; so abstract that it has no reality at all. Red, as it is to *mere* sense, unrelated by thought to other colors or to any other sensation, is something that only the fertile imagination of such men as John Stuart Mill can conceive. Red, *as we know it*, gets its distinctive character from the relations in which it stands, and the relations in which it stands are *logical* relations. This is, of course, the same old story that Professor T. H. Green told so often, but it bears repeating "because it so true," and because not every one has come to recognize its truth. Now as these relations are logical, logic has not

only the right, but also the duty, to consider what are generally called sensuous objects and all the relations in which they
stand; only it must not consider such objects as merely affec-
tions of sense, unelaborated by thought. Pure thought, as
logic deals with it, is, therefore, thought that refuses to take
into account the *abstractly* sensuous nature of things; and, if
you wish it, is abstract in so refusing to do. But such an
abstraction from an abstraction is a concrete view as well as
an abstraction, just as a negation of a negation is an affirmation as well as a negation.

That this, again, is Hegel's view and not my own subjective
interpretation, will appear upon reading a passage in that much
neglected Introduction to the *Greater Logic,* where Hegel has
expressed himself so clearly that I must be permitted to quote
the passage quite at large. In it the reader will notice that
Hegel, while recognizing the abstractness of logic and of
logical thought from one point of view, maintains that from a
higher point of view they are concrete. " Thus whoever
approaches the science finds in logic, at first, an isolated system of abstractions, which is restricted to itself and does not
reach over the other knowledges and sciences. Rather, contrasted with the riches of the presentative consciousness of the
world (*Weltvorstellung*), with the content of the other sciences,
which appears so real, and above all, with the promise of the
absolute science to unveil the *essence* of these riches, the *inner
nature* of spirit and of the world, in a word, to unveil the *truth,*
this science, in its abstract form, in the colorless, cold simplicity
of its pure categories, has the appearance of doing anything
rather than of keeping its promise, and of standing empty-
handed in the presence of these riches. The first acquaintance
with logic restricts its significance to itself. Its content
passes only for an isolated occupation with the categories,
besides which the other scientific occupations have an important matter and content of their own. . . . Thus, then, logic
must indeed be learned as something that one does well enough
to understand and get an insight into; but something in which
compass, depth, and further significance are at the beginning

lacking. It is only with a deeper knowledge of the other sciences, that, for the subjective spirit, the logical is raised to the rank of a universal; not a universal that is only abstract, but one that comprehends within itself the riches of the particular. . . . Now, although in the beginning of this study, the logical is not present to the spirit in this conscious power, still by this study the spirit receives into itself the power that leads it into all truth. The system of logic is the realm of shadows, the world of simple essences, freed from all sensuous concreteness. The study of this science, abode and work in this realm of shadows, is the absolute culture and discipline of consciousness. Therein is plied an occupation remote from sensuous perceptions and aims, from feelings, from the merely make-believe world of ordinary consciousness. Considered on its negative side, this occupation consists in keeping aloof from the contingency of sophistic thought and from the arbitrariness of letting this, that, or the other reason strike and prevail. By such study, however, thought wins self-reliance and independence. It becomes at home in the abstract and in procedure by conceptions without sensuous substrata; it becomes the unconscious power of taking up the alien manifold of the knowledges and sciences into the form of reason, of conceiving and keeping them in their essentiality, of stripping off the external, and, in this way, of extracting from them what is logical. To say the same thing in other words, it becomes the power of filling the abstract groundwork of the logical, previously acquired by the study of logic, with the content of all truth, and of giving it the value of a universal which no longer stands as a particular by the side of another particular, but reaches over this other particular and is its essence, the absolutely true." [1]

After what has been said, it will be easy to reply to the other criticism of Trendelenburg, that "*motion* is without more ado presupposed by the dialectic, which is to presuppose nothing." What moves, of course, has a sensuous aspect, but the efforts of modern experimental psychology have not yet suc-

[1] I, 43-45 (46-48).

ceeded in discovering a *sense* of motion (*pace* Professor James), any more than in discovering a sense of time or of space. And one might very well risk his reputation as a prophet on the prediction that such a discovery will never be made. Motion involves a synthesis, and the synthetic as synthetic can never be apprehended by mere sense. Kant's results on this point are likely to remain unshaken, and are available for us here, even though Kant himself did not apply them to the explanation of motion. Motion is a schematized category; and Kant would have classed it as such if only he had taken a wider view of the pure categories and had included Becoming among them. But the motion in Hegel's *Logic,* which has been the stone of stumbling and the rock of offence to his critics, is a category *not even schematized.* In spite of Trendelenburg's failure to find in Hegel any intimation that motion in logic is something different from motion in external nature, Hegel expressly repudiates any admixture of *time* in his logical Becoming, which he calls the motion of Being and Naught into each other. He objects to the popular proverbs that identify Being and Naught, on the ground that this identification is not made in the pure element of thought, but has its medium in time.[1] In this case, however, a word to the wise was not sufficient; and Trendelenburg and many after him have filled up their pages with the charge that in motion a false brother has been brought in unawares to spy out the liberty that the categories should have in the world of thought — to whom the critics will give place, no, not for an hour ! The truth is that it is the critics themselves who have brought in physical motion through their failure to read Hegel carefully. He states that he prefers the word ' becoming ' to the word 'transition ' (*Uebergehen*), because in the latter there is an implication that the *terminus a quo* and the *terminus ad quem* are external to each other, and the movement is represented as taking place *between* these fixed points.[2] If this fixity and mutual externality of points between which motion takes place

---

[1] I, 75 (80), " Seyn und Nichts werden in der Zeit auseinander gehalten."
[2] I, 87 (92, 93).

is not the characteristic of natural motion, it would be hard to characterize it.   And if the absence of this characteristic does not plainly indicate a motion that is not natural, it is for the critics to adduce a single instance of natural motion that is not thought of as characterized by just this trait.

What Hegel means by 'motion' in the dialectic is the timeless and spaceless synthesis of opposites in one eternal thought, in which they keep their distinctness, but in which such a logical interplay of these distinctions prevails, that the very essence of each is seen to consist in the character it gets · from its organic relation to the other.   Perhaps an illustration will help us to understand Hegel's thought, an illustration taken from one of the highest instances, in the world of nature, of that organic unity which, he says,[1] should characterize the system of categories.   The human hand, considered as a thing in space, has only a latent reference to all other things in space; but the *thought* of a human hand, as a hand, is really the thought of the *whole human body*, in which the hand is only an element.   Think the hand as it is in itself, in its own peculiar nature and conception, and you find that that very thought of the hand, which tries so hard to be peculiar, has transcended its peculiarity and become the thought of the body, in which the thought of the hand is only a moment or constitutive factor.   Now distinguish between the human hand and the human trunk in your thought, and you will discover that your distinction cannot widen into an absolute separation, without the loss, to each separate element, of its own character.   To use Hegel's language, " in their distinction they remain, each *in itself*, the whole concept."[2]   Each becomes the other, in that the thought of each is seen to involve the thought of the other.   But does each *change in time* from what it was in itself to what the other is in itself?   Assuredly not.   Time does not come into consideration here at all.   It is not that you first think the hand completely, and then proceed to think the trunk.   It is that the very thought of the hand, in the very act of self-realization, becomes the thought

[1] I, 31 (33).   [2] I, 48 (51).

of the trunk also — not two thoughts, here of a hand, there of a trunk, but one thought of a hand-and-trunk, which is neither hand alone nor trunk alone, but a body with organic distinctions in it.

Hegel's contention, then, is that the categories of thought are so inter-related that you cannot employ one of them without employing in that very act its antithesis. The employment of the antithesis is not a second act; but the first act proves, on inspection, not to be the employment of merely one category, nor the double employment of two categories, but the single employment of an organizing category, in which the so-called first and second categories are moments or distinctions. Now this turning out of a category not to be itself alone, but rather itself as a distinction against its opposite in the concrete unity that synthesizes them, — this turning out, I say, is not a temporal process, much less a spatial process, but is an eternal, unchanging truth. Movement can be predicated of it only as a "transferred epithet." It is the *student* who moves from the psychic state in which he is not consciously aware of the synthetic character of his thought, or perhaps it is more correct to say, in which he has not paid attention to the necessary logical environment of the category in which he is especially interested; and he advances to the psychic state in which the *tout ensemble* is an object of explicit knowledge because it has become an object of accurate attention. But this psychic time-movement is not a logical time-movement of the category itself. We must learn to divest words of their profane time and space associations and connotations, if we wish to take them with us into the holy sanctuary of logic. And Hegel is not guilty of the neglect of not pointing this out from time to time in the body of his *Greater Logic,* especially in the case of compound words in which the prepositional or adverbial component smacks strongly of time and space suggestions, as in the case of Transition [1] (*Uebergehen*) and of Determinate Being [2] (*Daseyn*). In other cases he takes for

[1] I, 87 (92, 93).
[2] I, 107 (113).

granted that his Preface to the second edition has been read, and the contents noted and remembered.

What has been said so far, may be summed up as follows: Logic presupposes the *Phenomenology*, and the *Phenomenology* presupposes ordinary consciousness with its sensuous cognition; and thus logic indirectly presupposes sensuous experiences. But it abstracts from the sensuous element in experience, because it has transcended the point of view from which the sensuous is regarded as an independent element standing over against thought. In logic the sensuous is considered only in so far as it has been intellectualized.

But now a reader of the *Greater Logic* will undoubtedly ask whether Hegel does not admit of beginning upon the study of logic without the preliminary discipline of the science of the phenomenal consciousness. Does he not give the option to the candidate for logical study either of orienting himself for logic by mastering the *Phenomenology*, or of merely making the arbitrary resolve to consider thought as such, and then of plunging immediately into the bacchic whirl of the categories? There is no question that Hegel proposes such an alternative;[1] but it may be worth while to see in what condition a candidate will find himself if he chooses the latter course. He will be one of those for whom logic is a science of mere abstractions; he will come to discover, to his great disappointment, that the bacchic dance is only an "unearthly ballet of bloodless categories." He will, in short, take the attitude that Mr. F. H. Bradley takes,[2] until he receives into himself "the power that leads into all truth." And the reason for this attitude is manifest. Such a resolve to consider thought as such, in its abstract purity, is, as Hegel himself says, thoroughly arbitrary — there is no necessity in it, considered as a merely psychological event. It is only a fact in the subjective history of the man who makes the resolve; and when in time it disappears, as all timed things must and all psychic things quickly do, then the logic that is built upon such a resolve

[1] I, 59 (63).
[2] *The Principles of Logic*, p. 533.

goes too. It will be as powerless to resist the seductions of
"that warm and breathing beauty of flesh which our hearts
find delightful," as was Hume's scepticism impotent against
some "lively impression of the senses, which obliterate all
these chimeras." It is only when the consideration of thought
as such is not the result of a capricious resolve, but is seen to
be the inevitable consequence of even the most sensuous consciousness, and when thought has taken into itself "all the
kingdoms of the world and the glory of them" instead of dealing with them as enticements from without — it is only then
that a logic that deals with pure thought does not appear a
"spectral woof of impalpable abstractions," but "leaves the
world more glorious."

And, besides, such a contingent resolve is itself a presupposition, and a very insecure presupposition upon which to found
an absolute science. It is true that, having such a presupposition, we can and must proceed, as Hegel shows, without any
other; and if we do so, we shall find that we must start with
pure Being. But to proceed without any further presupposition beyond an unnecessitated resolve, is not to start without
any presupposition. And this leads us back to the question
whether Hegel anywhere claims that his *Logic* is without presuppositions. After a careful and somewhat extended examination of Hegel's own statements and of his theory of logic,
we can now answer that question as we answered it in the
beginning of this enquiry. Hegel nowhere makes the claim
that this science is without presupposition. He explicitly says
the very contrary.

But what he does say, and what has been misunderstood
and misinterpreted into that, is that the *category with which
the logical movement begins* must be, at least apparently, without presupposition. The distinction and world-wide difference
between these two statements, the one that Hegel makes, and
the other that the critics say he makes, is so important to the
understanding of the dialectic, that we must drive home the
consciousness of it. To say that logic has no presuppositions
is to say that any one, no matter how immature, no matter

how "drunk in sense," can, just as he is, without any further growth, without any change of heart, begin the study of speculative logic. Hegel was not so foolish as to make any such statement. What he did say has already been quoted in part, and can be summed up by saying that no really *vital* study of logic can begin until the student is convinced of the necessity of the point of view of absolute knowledge. A rather formal, and yet by no means idle, study of logic, as a kind of propaedeutic to logic as a vital science, can be begun by any one who makes a really earnest resolve to deal with abstract thought. This resolve is a presupposition of the formal study; and such a successful prosecution of the formal study as will finally reveal to him the secret of absolute knowledge, is a further presupposition of the study of the living logical universal.

Having seen what Hegel did not say was without presupposition, let us now go on to see what he really did say was without presupposition; and let us try to see what he meant by such a claim. I will quote a few sentences. "The beginning must be an absolute, or, what is the same thing, an abstract beginning. It must presuppose nothing, must be mediated by nothing, and must have no ground." [1] "Neither is that beginning something arbitrary, something assumed merely for the nonce, nor is it something that appears as a capricious phenomenon or as a thing presupposed by leave, of which, however, the sequel shows that one did right in making it the beginning." [2] "What constitutes the beginning, the beginning itself, is to be taken, therefore, as something not analyzable, something in its simple, empty immediacy, such as *Being* or the absolutely void." [3]

This last sentence makes a good point of departure for the study of Hegel's meaning. The presupposition of logic is that there is such a thing as absolute knowledge, knowledge in which the elements are not brought together by an external force which simply brings them into juxtaposition, but in which every element is what it is by virtue of its relation

[1] I, 59 (63). [2] I, 61, 62 (66). [3] I, 65, 66 (70).

to the others in the unity of the absolute whole. If this view of the concrete, synthetic unity of thought is true, then it must be possible to take any category and show that it involves the whole system of categories; just as it was shown above that the conception of the human hand involves the conception of the whole human body. That is, there must be a science which traces the gradual unfolding of the implications of each category until that category is seen only as a moment in the ultimate unity of the Absolute Idea. The question is: Where must this science begin? Evidently, if it is to do its work thoroughly, it must begin, not at some rather fully developed category, but at the lowest category. It is a matter, not of choice, but of necessity; and the necessity is imposed by the very idea of the science. For the science is to be the exhibition of the organic unity of all the categories. Hence all the categories must be discussed if the science is to be complete; and as it is the science that exhibits the truth that every category in itself involves every other category, the only orderly procedure is to begin with that category which seems farthest removed from any such implication. Now the category that seems least to involve the organic unity to which it belongs must be the one that bears in itself the least trace of being organic — *it must be simple and unanalyzable,* at least in appearance; for whatever is itself a unity of distinctions may more easily be a distinction within a higher unity, than what seems to be a bare blank identity without distinctions. In other words an organism has this peculiarity, that every member in it is an organism also, and what is not itself organic cannot have an integral place within a higher organic individual.

If this is true, then the science that undertakes to exhibit the organic nature and unity of the system of categories must show the organic nature of each single category; and it must begin, in order to be systematic, with the category which has the least trace of such an organic nature. And as the organic nature of the Absolute Idea, of which they are all to be proved members, is a unity of distinctions into which it may be analyzed, then the category that, on the face of it, is absolutely simple and without distinctions must be the category to begin with. Is there such a category? It seems that we have it in the conception of pure Being. Starting, then, with this category of seemingly absolute simplicity, we are bound to show that it is not so simple as it seems, if we are to maintain our conception of the organic unity of all the categories. Thus, we see that the very nature of the task that logic sets before itself makes it necessary that it should begin with the conception that claims to be unanalyzable, to be simple, to have no elements, or, what is the same thing, no presuppositions; for the presuppositions of a category in the dialectic are the elements or moments that constitute the synthetic unity of that category. Now of all the categories that we use, there are none that can lay such plausible claim to being simple, as pure Being and pure Naught. The choice lies between the two; and dialectical considerations, that is, considerations determined by the very nature of the process that constitutes the principle of the logical science, decide the issue in favor of pure Being.

This, then, is the proper place to examine the criticism that Naught, and not Being, should be the starting-point of such a dialectical development. This criticism was made in Hegel's lifetime, and in the second edition of his *Greater Logic* he notices it.[1] He maintains that the only consideration that can determine one to accept Naught as the emptiest category is one of merely external reflection, "an external play of abstraction." In other words, it is only when you set the negative and the positive side by side in an external way, that it seems that the negative is more empty and unanalyzable than the positive. For the presentative consciousness (*Vorstellung*), the negative is the more empty; but for the thinking or logical consciousness, the negative is the fuller. For when you reflect that the thought of the negative has as an element in it the thought of that which it negates, you see that the negative, when *thought*, must presuppose the positive; but it is not so easily seen that the positive presupposes the negative. To

[1] I, 95, 96 (100–102).

say the same thing in another way, if the positive presupposes the negative, the presupposition is *implicit* and *latent*, and difficult to bring before the attention. But the negative presupposes the positive *explicitly*, and has no semblance of a meaning except as containing the positive as a moment within it. Hence Being, the positive, appears to be more simple and unanalyzable than Naught, the negative.

I have thus shown what Hegel means by saying the beginning for logic or within logic must be without presupposition. Explicit statements have been adduced to show that my explanation is not forced, but is merely an amplification of what Hegel himself says. But if the reader is still not satisfied, I ask him to examine the reasons Hegel gives for not accepting some of the other initial categories proposed. He passes in review the suggestions that the first category should be *Beginning, Subject-matter, I.* His objection in every case is either that the proposed substitute is nothing but another name for pure Being, or that it is evidently a unity of distinctions and consequently *analyzable.* It may be well to quote what he says with regard to beginning with the category of *Beginning.* " It is still Naught, and is to be something. The Beginning is not pure Naught, but a Naught out of which something is to proceed. Being is thus already contained in Beginning. Beginning contains both Being and Naught — or it is Non-being that is at the same time Being, and Being that is at the same time Non-being." [1] He carries this train of reflection on through four paragraphs, the gist of all which is that Beginning, *as admitting of analysis*, must be rejected as not the initial category. Again, what he says against *I* (*ego*) as an applicant for the first position is equally significant: " *I* in general, however, is also at the same time a concrete category, or, rather, it is the most concrete of all — the consciousness of self as of an infinitely manifold world. For making *I* the beginning and the ground of philosophy, it is imperative to eliminate this concrete content." [2]

[1] I, 63, 64 (68).
[2] I, 66 (71).

Thus, whether we look at what Hegel says positively as to the presuppositionlessness of the initial category he has chosen, or at what he says negatively, as against categories that apply for the first place in the dialectic, we see clearly that by the demand that the beginning of logic should have no presupposition, is meant that the *initial category should be the most simple, unanalyzable conception,* containing within it no explicit reference to any other category. All considerations, thus far, therefore, indicate pure Being as the point of departure for the dialectical development.

But I have not yet given the subtlest argument that Hegel advances in support of his procedure in beginning with this category. What has been given is to some extent not an exhibition of the *unconditioned* necessity of starting at this point. For it was only after a search that we discovered pure Being to be the most available applicant.

It is at this point again, as at so many others, that the conception of pure knowledge, pure thought, comes to the logician's aid. The presupposition of the *Logic* can be made to discover, without contingency or failure, the presuppositionless category. I have already quoted at length the passage in the enquiry, "With what must the Science begin?" in which Hegel shows that it must begin with the results reached by the *Phenomenology.* If the reader will refer to the passage,[1] read it over again, and then read what is now to be quoted, — a continuation of that passage, — he will see the train of thought and the meaning of Hegel.

"Now that, from the standpoint of this conception of pure knowledge, the beginning remains immanent, there is nothing to do but consider that pure knowledge, or, rather, setting aside all reflections, all opinions that we may otherwise have, there is nothing to do but only take *what is before us.*

"Pure knowledge, *as having consolidated into this unity,* has sublated all reference to an other and to mediation; it is the distinctionless; this distinctionless thing ceases therewith to be even knowledge; there is only *simple immediacy* present.

[1] See above, p. 503.

Simple immediacy is itself an expression of a category of reflection, and implies a distinction from what is mediated. Hence, in its true expression, this simple immediacy is *pure Being*." [1]

Perhaps a little comment on this passage may help to clear away all obscurity. Logic, as a fruitful science, begins at the point in our philosophical career where we have come to see that knowledge and its object are not opposed, but are one with each other. Knowledge is the all, which includes its object, and is not mediated by it, as if it were something really other than it. In such logic, therefore, we cannot begin with an object as distinct from knowledge, but must begin with knowledge *knowing itself*. The beginning must be immanent within thought, and we must take merely what we find in that conception of pure knowledge or pure thought, as our beginning. We thus find that we must begin with the conception of *simple immediacy;* for if there is no reference to an other in the thought that we are dealing with, there is only immediacy and simplicity present. But the term 'simple immediacy' is not a very happy term to use here, because it is not the expression of what we wish to express. 'Immediacy' is a negative term, and, like all negative terms, gets all its import from its contrast with mediation. We wish to express a thought that does *not* get its import from something else; that is, we want some word to express the category that is really *presuppositionless*. ' Pure Being ' is the term we want. Now, of course, the verbal symbol is contingent. Because we are not Germans, we do not call it *das reine Seyn*, as Hegel did. But the category of the presuppositionless is forced on us as the initial category of our logic, by virtue of the presupposition with which we came to the subject.

We must remember, therefore, that when Hegel uses the term 'pure Being,' he uses it in the sense of the category of thought-thinking-self, without even distinguishing any moments within itself; for it is just beginning to think itself, without yet seeing of what further nature the self that it thinks is. It has a further nature, as will presently appear; but at the begin-

[1] I, 58 (62).

ning of this thought, the only trait that appears is this empty thinking, which is well expressed by 'pure Being.'

These, then, are the two considerations that led Hegel to begin his dialectical movement with pure Being; or, as he would have preferred to say, these are the facts in the subject-matter with which Logic deals, that make it necessary that the science should begin with this category. The one fact is that, as the science is to show the organic relation in which every category stands to all-inclusive thought, this exhibition must begin with that category which seems to stand infinitely removed from such an organic unity; and in its progress it must sweep the road it traverses, along with it, into the goal it reaches. The other fact is that in this science thought begins to think thought, and must therefore begin with the category which is proper to this commencement of pure self-realization, namely, the category of pure Being.

This method of Hegel's for justifying his beginning — how unlike it is to the methods attributed to him by his critics! Some think that they see mere arbitrariness in his choice of point of departure. He is made to say: "Let Being be the starting-place," and it is the starting-place. But this is almost as good as the way in which Mr. McTaggart, again working from the *Encyclopaedia* and apparently ignoring the *Greater Logic*, tries to justify the ways of Hegel to men. "Now the idea from which the dialectic sets out, and in which it professes to show that all the other categories are involved, is the idea of Being. Are we justified in assuming the validity of this idea? The ground on which we can answer this question in the affirmative is that the rejection of the idea as invalid would be self-contradictory, as was pointed out above. For it would be equivalent to the denial that anything whatever existed. And in that case the denial itself could not exist, and the validity of the idea of Being has not been denied." [1] " This is, of course, the Cartesian argument, which is never stated by Hegel precisely in this form, but on which the justi-fication of his use of the category of Being, as valid of reality,

[1] *Op. cit.*, p. 90.

appears to depend." [1]   This would be well enough if Hegel began his *Logic* with the category of Actual Existence (*Wirklichkeit*) — but perhaps I should not concede even so much. It would be well enough as a justification for a *phenomenological* and not a *logical* development from that point.   And, besides, Mr. McTaggart would find it hard to convince a sceptic by any Cartesian process that the existence of his denial proved the existence of *pure* Being; and Descartes would have made a worse case of it than he did, if he had taken as his argument, *Cogito, ergo ens purum et abstractum sum.*   Hegel found that it took some five hundred pages of the *Phenomenology* to raise an empirical sceptic to the point where he could see that the existence of anything involved pure Being, and he found that he could do it only by making thought so ungrateful as to swallow up the 'datum' from which it set out.   In other words, Hegel saw clearly that it was only upon the presupposition of an *absolute* thought, of which his commentator denies the possibility, that pure Being could be shown to be involved in the existence of any psychic fact, and so in a *denial* of pure Being.   It is hard to see how Mr. McTaggart, with his knowledge of the *Encyclopaedia,* could suppose that he is justifying the category of *pure* Being by pointing to an object (the psychic state of denial) which is thought under the category of Actuality.   It is a far cry from the first category in Being to an advanced one in Essence. Hegel's justification of his use of the category of Being as valid of reality could not very well rest upon a confusion of pure Being with actual concrete existence.   It could rest only on the insight that in the last analysis what appears to have an existence independent of thought is really not independent of thought, but is of the very constitution of thought; that thought thus has no counterpart to itself, but exhausts the whole of reality — in a word that thought is *pure* and *absolute.*   The category under which we think this unconditionality of thought is the category of *pure Being.*

[1] *Op. cit.,* p. 21.

THE

PRINCIPLE 'AND THE METHOD

OF THE

HEGELIAN DIALECTIC

A DEFENCE OF THE DIALECTIC
AGAINST ITS CRITICS

BEING A

THESIS ACCEPTED BY THE FACULTY OF THE COLLEGE OF LETTERS
IN THE UNIVERSITY OF CALIFORNIA IN PART FULFILMENT
OF THE REQUIREMENTS FOR THE DEGREE OF
DOCTOR OF PHILOSOPHY

BY

EVANDER BRADLEY McGILVARY

PART II

THE METHOD OF THE DIALECTIC

Reprinted from MIND, New Series, Vol. VII, No. 25 and 26

BERKELEY
UNIVERSITY OF CALIFORNIA
1897

THE DIALECTICAL METHOD. (I.)

[*Off-printed from* MIND: *a Quarterly Review of Psychology and Philosophy. Vol. VII., N.S., No. 25.*]

BY PROF. E. B. McGILVARY.

IN this paper I shall consider, as far as I may, the objections that have been raised against the method of the Hegelian dialectic, with a view to determine what is the real nature of that method. And in doing this I shall avail myself, in great part, of Mr. McTaggart's chapter on the development of the method of the dialectic,[1] as a convenient and accessible statement of the views against which I wish to protest as being unhegelian. It matters not that he presents his views as a sympathiser with Hegel rather than as an opponent. The views call for such a discussion as will bear equally against an adverse school of criticism, which has flourished upon a misunderstanding of the method it criticises. Even where Mr. McTaggart's contentions are fire-new, as in his claim that the negative is not essential to the movement of the dialectic, what he says will make a good basis upon which to treat the subject of the negative in its relation to the dialectic, a favourite subject of the critics.

If there is any work, the results of which depend entirely upon *the integrity of the method* employed, that work is Hegel's *Logic*. Indeed, the method is more important and more secure than the results in their detail, and no one knew this better than its author. In the Introduction to his *Greater Logic*, he calls the method "the soul of the structure,"[2] and says of it: "Although I could not possibly

---

[1] *Studies in the Hegelian Dialectic*, by John McTaggart Ellis McTaggart, M.A., Fellow of Trinity College, Cambridge. Cambridge: at the University Press, 1896. Chapter IV. Part of the work appeared in a series of articles in MIND (New Series, Nos. 1, 2, 8, and 10).

[2] Hegel's *Wissenschaft der Logik*, i., 42 (45). In my reference to this work I follow the pagination of the reissue of 1841, from the press of Duncker & Humblot, Berlin; giving in parenthesis the paging of the first issue. The three volumes of the *Logic* form the third, fourth and fifth volumes of the *Complete Works*. I use the *Greater Logic* rather than the *Lesser*, partly because it is a fuller treatment of the whole

think that the method which I have pursued—or rather which this system pursues of itself—might not be capable of much perfecting, of much thorough revising in its details, I know, nevertheless, that it is the only true method. This is clear of itself already from the fact that it is nowise distinct from its object and content; for it is the content in itself, it is *the dialectic that the content has within it*, which moves the content forward. It is clear that no treatment can pass for scientific that does not go the gait of this method and conform to its simple rhythm, for it is the gait of the subject-matter itself." [1]

Against this, Mr. McTaggart claims that the method is not uniform, but is constantly changing, and that the change is of two kinds: first, from external reflexion, which alone is at work in the categories of Being, through various intermediate forms, till at the last inner reflexion gets in its hand; secondly, that the negative is not an essential element in the method, but functions only in its earlier stages and gradually disappears altogether from the scene of action.

I. I shall begin with the first point made, namely, that external reflexion is the power that moves the machinery in the categories of Being as over against those of Essence and of Conception. His statement is this: " In Being each category appears, taken by itself, to be permanent and exclusive of all others, and to have no principle of transition in it. It is only outside reflexion which examines and breaks down this pretence of stability, and shows us that the dialectic process is inevitable. In Essence, however, each category by its own import refers to that which follows it, and the transition is seen to be inherent in its nature. But it is still felt to be, as it were, only an external effect of that nature. The categories have still an inner nature, as contrasted with the outer relations which they have with the other categories. So far as they have this inner nature, they are still conceived as independent and self-centred. But with the passage into the notion things alter ; that passage 'is the very hardest, because it proposes that independent actuality shall be thought as having all its substantiality in the passing over and identity with the other

subject ; partly because it is not so familiar to English readers, and thus will throw new light on the points discussed ; and partly because the first volume of the *Greater Logic*, which concerns us most especially in the present paper, *is the latest work from Hegel's pen*, and therefore represents his matured views better than the *Logic* of the *Encyclopædia*.

[1] I., 39 (41, 42).

independent actuality '.[1] Not only is the transition now necessary to the categories, but the transition *is* the categories. The reality in any finite category, in this stage, consists only in its summing up those which went before, and in leading on to those which come after." [2]

Now, before we can satisfactorily enter upon a discussion of this point, it will be necessary to make some preliminary remarks about the *double aspect* in which the categories appear in the *Logic*. The primary purpose of the *Logic* is to show how even the most abstract and seemingly independent and inorganic category contains within itself the life of the whole system of all-inclusive Thought; and how this life, if allowed full play, will develop that barren category through all the stages of thought up to the highest. Now, as this category grows under our observation, we see it taking the form of other categories familiar to us. Thus in the very development of the lowest category we reach other categories whose evolution it is the business of logic to display. Hence it is not necessary to give a separate genealogical table to each category; but the pedigree of one category will be the pedigree of many—but, from one point of view,[3] *not the pedigree of all*. And this is an important point. There are categories that, in the form in which we ordinarily use them, or rather in which we *think* we use them, are not to be found in the direct line of march from pure Being towards the goal of the Absolute Idea. But though not on the line of march, they are near by, and it takes only a little flank movement to sweep them into it. But this flank movement arrests the procession "for the subjective spirit," as Hegel would say. It *appears as if* there were a zigzag movement with constant stops, and not a "never-halting march".[4]

I may illustrate what I mean by borrowing and developing the metaphor Hegel uses for representing the absolute unity of thought. This unity is a circle; thought's movement is in an orbit that returns upon itself. But suppose that one has not yet discovered the orbit, does not even know whether there be any orbit or any movement; suppose one loses one's perspective, and, from any position, views two points in the circumference of the circle. These points

---

[1] "*Enc.*, Section 159."

[2] *Op. cit.*, pp. 123, 124.

[3] I wish to call especial attention to this reservation. For, from another point of view, it *is* the pedigree of all.

[4] I., 39 (41): "In unaufhaltsamem . . . Gange".

may appear to him *side by side,* rather than *one in advance of the other.* The more advanced point is then viewed as if it were collateral with the nearer ; hence when a movement is discovered and is supposed to be in a bee-line from the point of observation through one of these points on to the infinite, it will seem as though a digression must be made from this line in order to catch the other point into the movement. In the same way a higher category is viewed as if it were co-ordinate with a lower one ; so viewed, it will not have all the characteristics it should have, else it would not appear co-ordinate. In such a case, it is clear that when the lower category has advanced to the higher, it will not have passed through the form the higher takes *when reduced to a lower plane.* Now, as ordinary thought is abstract and thinks its categories in their abstractness, and not in their concreteness, it will be necessary, when dialectic comes alongside of a category in its abstract form, to show how this abstract category develops itself into the same concrete fulness into which its seeming co-ordinate was developed. To change the figure, the stone which, in the structure of speculative logic, has its significance only as resting on the lower stones and furnishing a basis for the higher, is by the common thinker torn out of its place and used as an independent unit. It is the business of the speculative builder, when he reaches this stone in its structural place, to show that even when lying apart it bears traces upon itself that cannot fail to indicate that such isolation is not proper to it, but that it belongs to an architectural system ; and to show that these traces also indicate *where* it belongs in that system.

But even this is not all. ,Common understanding has its own ways of artificially grouping these abstract categories. One way, and a very favourite way, especially in dealing with the categories that dialectic reaches first, is to pair them off, and to set each member of a pair over against the other, as of equal rank, but mutually incompatible. Thus from the abstract point of view, these paired-off categories are contradictory to each other ; and what dialectic does, appears to be a reconciling of these contradictions. When Hegel, therefore, speaks of any category " as such," he means that category regarded as the " unspeculative " thinker regards it ; that is, as leading to no dialectical result, and even as independent of the process by which speculative logic has reached it. And when he speaks of its " opposite," he means, in the lower categories, what the abstract thinker regards as its irreconcilable contradictory ; and when he speaks of " reconciling " these contradictories, he is merely using language that repre-

sents the view of abstract thought. Dialectic, however, does
not recognise the claims of the opposites to be incompatible,
and hence need perform no atoning work. To put this in
technical Hegelian language, it is merely *external reflexion*
that regards the speculative logic as reconciling contradictories. Logic itself, in performing this operation which
an onlooker calls a reconciliation, is not conscious of being
engaged in a ministry of reconciliation, but is only conscious
of advancing from a lower to a higher category.

What I have said above may easily be misunderstood; for
it may seem to imply that the higher category is not a unity
of *opposites*. It *is* such a unity, but not of *contradictory*
opposites, or of *contrary* opposites, *as these terms are used in
the traditional logic;* and it is this fact that I have wished to
make prominent, and I may be thought to have carried the
emphasis on to the point of danger. To put it all in one
sentence, logic takes what appear to be contradictories, and
does what appears to be a reconciling of them; but succeeds
in so doing, merely because they are not *such* contradictories
as cannot be thought together in one thought.

The best proof of the correctness of this exposition is the
light that it throws upon many a dark passage in Hegel's
Logic. If we bear in mind the double aspect of the negative
categories, we shall be able to solve riddles that otherwise
would remain insoluble, except by the Gordian-knot method
to which Mr. McTaggart has resorted. I shall quote one passage of the many that find their explanation only in what has
just been said. In the *Greater Logic*, under the section,
Determinate Being as Such, there is a sub-section, *Determinate Being in General*. Here we read: "Determinate Being
arises out of Becoming. Determinate Being is the simple
unity of Being and Naught. Because of this simplicity, it
has the form of an *immediate*. Its mediation, Becoming, lies
behind it, has been sublated. Determinate Being, therefore,
appears as a primal datum from which we take our start."[1]
Here it is evident that Hegel is not concerned with determinate Being *as it has been mediated*—that is, as it appears
to the speculative thinker—but as it appears *apart from* its
mediation. He seems to be giving an answer, not to the
question how this category has arisen in the course of the
dialectical process, but to the question how it comes that, if
it has thus arisen, it appears *un*mediated. The answer is
that the process lies behind the category, and the unspeculative thinker does not look behind for it, but looks only at

[1] L., 106 and 107 (112 and 113).

what lies immediately before him. It is true that there is some
excuse for such neglect on the part of the thinker; for, in
one sense, this category, as well as every other, is immediate
even from the point of view of the speculative thinker; for
immediacy is not a characteristic on the same level with
mediation and antagonistic to it. Like all true dialectical
negatives, it is higher than that which it negates, containing
mediateness as one of its moments. In this sense immediacy is self-mediation; and it is in this sense that determinate Being is for the speculative thinker immediate; for its
presuppositions, its moments, its media are *in* it and not *behind* it. This is one of the things that Hegel means when
he says that in this category mediation is sublated; for to
sublate means both to cancel and to retain. Mediation is
cancelled, for this category is immediate; and it is retained,
for this category is, from a higher point of view, self-
mediated. But a full insight into this truth does not yet
appear, and it would be anticipating a later result of the dialectic to bring forth this truth at this stage. This revelation
will be made first by the category of Being-for-self. Hence
the real purpose of introducing determinate Being as *immediate* and of saying that it appears as a new starting-point,
is to account for the apparent immediacy of the category *as
it is ordinarily regarded*.

We are now ready to return to the discussion upon which
we entered on the second page of this paper, and to examine
the claim made by Mr. McTaggart, that in the categories of
Being the dialectic advance is made possible only by outer
reflexion. And the first thing to do is to determine the
meaning of the expression " outer reflexion ". It is a phrase
constantly used by Hegel in his *Logic*, and fully explained in
the Second Book;[1] but it will not be necessary to quote and
to explain this difficult passage, for I do not intend to give
an outline of Hegel's doctrine of reflexion, but merely to
touch upon such features of this doctrine, or rather upon
such corollaries from it, as bear upon our present purpose.
It does not concern us to investigate the true dialectical
relation between the different kinds of reflexion, but merely
to ascertain what Hegel means when he denies that outer
reflexion is the motive power in the earlier categories, and
what Mr. McTaggart presumably means when he asserts
that it is the only means used to secure the dialectical
advance in these categories.

Outer reflexion is a way of regarding two categories as

---

[1] II., 19 (19), *seq.*

having no genetic relation to each other, but as merely co-existing in the thinker's mind independently of each other. This thinker, as a third party, compares the categories and passes judgment upon them as to resemblance or difference. This judgment does not affect the true inner nature of the categories, but merely records the impression they make on an onlooker. For a corroboration of this description of the function of outer reflexion, I shall quote two passages from the First Book of the *Greater Logic*; for it is this book that deals with the categories now in question. In one passage Hegel says: "This sameness of the determinations" (of Something and Other) "is only a matter of outer reflexion, of comparison of the two".[1] Here we see an identification of outer reflexion and comparison. The second passage is more explicit. "We have still," says he, "to mention particularly the word *unity*, which is, if I may say so, very infelicitous. It designates, even more than *identity* does, a subjective reflexion; for it is for the most part considered as a relation that arises from *comparison*, from external reflexion. In as far as this faculty finds the same characteristic in two *different objects*, a unity is present in such wise that, withal, there is also presupposed the complete *indifference* to this unity on the part of the objects themselves that are compared. The act of comparing, therefore, and the unity do not concern the objects themselves at all, but are an activity and a determination external to them."[2] External or outer reflexion, then, brings together two categories considered as mutually independent, and establishes a relation between them for its own convenience; but this relation is not regarded as in any way arising from their true inner nature, or as in any way affecting that nature. *Inner reflexion* is opposed to this outer reflexion.[3] What this inner reflexion is can be seen by studying the passage in the Introduction to the *Greater Logic*, where Hegel says that "the divisions and headings of the books, sections and chapters . . . do not belong to the contents and body of the science, but are arrangements of outer reflexion. . . . They are meant to have no other significance than that of a table of contents. But, besides, the *necessity* of the connexion" (of the categories thus brought together externally) "and the *immanent origin* of the distinctions are found in the treatment of the subject-matter itself; for they are involved in the progressive self-determination of the conception. That by which the conception accomplishes its self-advance-

[1] I., 117 (123).   [2] I., 84 and 85 (90).   [3] I., 94 (100).

ment is the aforesaid *negative*, that it has in it. This constitutes the truly dialectical feature. . . . Ordinarily the dialectic is regarded as an external and negative activity, that does not belong to the subject-matter itself. This activity is supposed to have its source in mere vain caprice, acting as a subjective impulse to take what is firm and true and make it totter and fall to pieces."[1] Here the contrast between outer and inner reflexion is clearly stated, although inner reflexion is not mentioned by name. While in outer reflexion the relation between two categories is established, not by the categories themselves, but by an *outsider*, in inner reflexion one category is seen to rise inevitably out of the other by immanent necessity, by reason of the negative that resides in the other. "Outside reflexion" is therefore *subjective*, and is contingent on the attitude of an outsider. Inner reflexion is *objective*, and is necessary from the very inner constitution of the object.

With the *caveat* already entered, that I am here treating of outer and of inner reflexion only in their bearing upon my present purpose, and not in their dialectical relations to each other, I am now ready to examine Mr. McTaggart's assertion that, in the categories of Being, "it is only outside reflexion which . . . shows us that the dialectical process is inevitable". But as he maintains that the process throughout Being is not uniform, so he would perhaps say that the kind of reflexion involved in the advance changes with the advance, and that if we want a typical instance of the enginery used in Being, we must take up the very first triad. So be it. If we can prove that the advance here is not due to outer reflexion, *a fortiori* we may conclude that *nowhere* is it due to outer reflexion.

Hegel himself realises the difficulty of getting a start. This difficulty lies in the fact that we must begin with an immediate category, with one that has not arisen from any other; for if it has so arisen it is no longer the first category, but its source is a category prior to it. But any immediate category must be simple; it may have no moments or constitutive factors; else it would not be immediate, but would be mediated by these moments.[2] But if it has no moments it would seem as if it must be a dead self-identity; and any progress from the category could not therefore be ac-

---

[1] I., 39-41 (42 and 43).

[2] I have discussed this point quite at length in an article on "The Presupposition Question in Hegel's Logic" in the *Philosophical Review*, September, 1897, pp. 512 *seq*.

complished by any indwelling motive power, but must be due to power from some external source. The advance is forced upon it from outside and is in no sense its own act.

This, then, is the apparent dilemma that Hegel had to face: Either there are moments immanent in the first category or there are none. If there are, then the first category is *not* the first category. If there are none, then the movement must be due to *external* reflexion, and is not a necessary logical movement at all. Hegel, however, evidently believed that this dilemma was more apparent than real; for on the very page of his *Greater Logic* where he calls attention to the fact that the transition in the first triad appears different from the subsequent transitions [1] he states that inner reflexion is at work here as well as outer reflexion ; and we shall soon see that inner reflexion is the true organon of the dialectical movement, and that outer reflexion is appealed to for the reason that we are dealing with categories appearing in a form not amenable to dialectic, because not capable of being thought. As they are not thought-determinations at all when appearing in this form, but are mere make-believes, their spurious character must be shown by the faculty of make-believe, that is, by external reflexion. Even the very way in which the two kinds of reflexion are spoken of here, shows which is the active power. Hegel is saying to his unspeculative opponent, who wants to test everything by outer reflexion: "Your own outer reflexion, as well as the inner reflexion proper to logic, sets down the indefiniteness of pure Being as equal to Naught, and declares it to be a mere creation of thought, a nothing".[2] Thus we see that, in the very first triad, he shows, in the most unmistakable way, his belief that inner reflexion is the vehicle of progress.

Let us now see whether we can discover how he justifies to himself such an escape from the apparent dilemma that confronts him. His statement of the difference which appears between the transition from the first to the second category, and all the later transitions, is this : "In the pure reflexion of the beginning, such as is made in this Logic with Being as such, the transition is still hidden. Because Being is only posited as immediate, Naught breaks forth into view in it only immediately. But all the follow-

---

[1] I., 94 (100).

[2] *Ibid.*, " Diese Unbestimmtheit oder abstracte Negation, welche so das Seyn an ihm selbst hat, ist es, was die äussere wie die innere Reflexion ausspricht, indem sie es dem Nichts gleich setzt ".

ing categories, *e.g.*, determinate Being, are more concrete "
(*i.e.*, complex, made up of factors). " There has already
been *explicitly posited* in them the element that contains
and produces the contradictions of those abstractions, and
therefore contains and produces their transition. In Being
as simple and immediate, the recollection that it is the
result of complete abstraction and thus is already abstract
negativity or Naught, has been laid aside before entering
upon our science. But in the course of the science, expressly from Essence onward, that one-sided *immediacy* will
be shown to be mediated ; for there Being appears as
Existence,[1] and the mediating factor of this Being, the
Ground, is *explicitly posited*." [2]

Again in another place he says : " We may still make
another remark about the character of the transition of
Being and Naught into each other, namely, that this transition is to be conceived without the help of any further
categories of reflexion. It is immediate and entirely abstract, because of the abstraction of the transitive moments,
that is, because there has not been explicitly posited in
either of these moments the determinateness of the other,
by means of which the transition could be effected. Naught
is not yet *posited* in Being, although Being is *essentially*
Naught, and *vice versâ*. Hence it is not permissible to
apply here principles of mediation which are further determined, and to conceive of Being and Naught as in some
essential relation (Verhältniss)—the transition is not as yet
an essential relation. It is thus not proper to say : ' Naught
is the *ground* of Being, or Being is the *ground* of Naught ' ;
or to say, ' Naught is the *cause* of Being, and so forth ' ; or
again to say : ' There can be transition into Naught only
under the condition that something *is*, or into Being only
under the condition of Non-Being '. The kind of relation
(Beziehung) cannot be further determined without further
determining at the same time the related sides. The nexus
of Ground and Consequence, for instance, no longer has for
its connected sides mere Being and Naught, but it has " (as
one side) " expressly Being that is Ground, and " (as the
other side) " something which is indeed only posited, not
independent, but something which is not abstract Naught," [3]
because abstract Naught *is* independent.

---

[1] Here let the reader bear in mind the etymology of this word, *ex-
sistentia*, a standing forth *out of* something as its ground. It is Being in
an *essential relation*.

[2] I., 94 and 95 (100).   [3] I., 99 and 100 (105 and 106).

And once again, at the end of the completed work, where he reviews the whole dialectical procedure in the light of the final result, he says: "The beginning has, accordingly, for this method no other characterisation than that it is the simple and universal. . . . The universal, however, in the absolute method, is not regarded as a mere abstract, but as the objective universal, that is, as that which *of itself* (an sich) *is the concrete totality*, but a totality not yet explicitly *posited*, not yet *for itself*" (*i.e.*, not yet explicitly recognised). "Even the abstract universal as such is in its concept, that is, considered in its truth, not merely the *simple;* but as *abstract* it is already *explicitly posited* as infected with *negation.* There is, therefore, whether in reality or in thought, nothing so simple and so abstract as one usually supposes. Such a simple is a mere *make-believe*, which has its ground only in the unconsciousness of what is in fact present. The initial category has been previously characterised as the immediate; this *immediacy of the universal* is the very same thing that is here expressed as that which is *of itself*, without being *for itself*. . . . The concrete totality which makes the beginning has, as such, in itself (in ihr selbst) the beginning of the advance and of the development. It is, as concrete, *possessed of distinctions within itself* (in sich unterschieden). Because of its *first immediacy*, however, the first distinct elements are at first *different*. However, the immediate, as self-referred universality, as subject, is also the *unity* of these different elements. This reflexion is the first stage of the advance, the emergence of *difference, judgment,*[1] *determination.* The essential thing is that the absolute method finds and recognises the determination of the universal in the universal itself. The finite knowledge of the understanding proceeds, in the act of determination, in the following way: what it laid aside in the creation of the universal by abstraction, it takes up again from the concrete in just as external a manner. On the contrary, the absolute method does not conduct itself as external reflexion, but gets the determinate out of the object itself, seeing that the method is the very immanent principle and soul of the object."[2]

I have made these many long quotations because the

---

[1] Hegel's use of "Urtheil" is peculiar, and, for the beginner, is puzzling. He takes it in the sense of a *self-originated diremption* of a concept; and it should, perhaps, be so translated here.

[2] III., 323-326 (333-335), quoted, as the asterisks show, with large omissions.

point they are meant to support is so important, and that point is this. Although the first category appears as simple and abstract, it is not so in *reality*, and the negation which seems to stand beside it as a mere indifferent neighbour is, in fact, "bone of its bone and flesh of its flesh," an Eve created out of the rib of Adam. But this immanent origin does not make itself manifest in the beginning; or, to use Hegel's own language just quoted, "in the pure reflexion of the beginning the transition is still hidden". At that stage, then, all that one can say is, that "Naught breaks forth into view in Being only immediately". There seems, as yet, to be no mediation for it on the part either of Being or of some third and external agent. We are not yet in a position to say that the emergence of the category Naught is due either to outer or to inner reflexion.[1] Just as the first category is taken in its immediacy, so the second is, at this point, to be considered as immediate. But just as further on we shall see that our first category is not immediate to the exclusion of mediation, but is mediated and *self*-mediated, so we shall see that the movement from the first category, which surprises us now because we cannot see any mediation for it, is mediated by the very moments which we shall find to mediate Being. As soon as Being shows itself up as not simple but complex, the apparently immediate emergence of the thought of Naught upon the thought of Being shows itself to be brought about by the originally hidden, but actually present, complex factors of Being. The transition is, then, really made by virtue of the negative that lurks unseen in pure Being; but because the negative is at present in hiding, the act of transition is also hidden.

There are thus three different kinds of reflexion that may deal with the relation existing between the categories of the first triad—*pure* reflexion, *external* reflexion and *internal* reflexion. Let us now proceed to see in detail how each kind of reflexion will exhibit the relation and how Hegel expresses the result obtained by each.

1. *Pure* reflexion puts the relation thus: "Because Being is only posited as immediate, Naught breaks forth into view in it only immediately. The transition is as yet hidden." This is Hegel's own way of representing the point of view of

---

[1] It is this inability to say anything as yet about the mediation of Naught, that makes Hegel call the reflexion at this stage "*pure reflexion*" (*In der reinen Reflexion des Anfangs*, i., 94 (100)). "Pure" here means two things. It means "not *externally* mediated," and also "*apparently not mediated at all*". It has the same meanings when used with Being and Naught, as will appear presently.

pure reflexion.[1] To express the same idea more fully, we should say that the thought (category) of Being can never be thought alone; but in thinking it we discover that we are always at the same time thinking the thought (category) of Naught. Neither Being alone, nor Naught alone, ever exhausts the content of the thought that thinks either; but both must be thought together in one synthetic thought. The conception of Naught is thus to be perceived in the conception of Being.[2] In the concept of Being, in the thought that clutches it, there is also present, clutched in the very same grip, another element, namely Naught. This is what Hegel means in the passage quoted above,[3] when he says: "Even the abstract universal as such is, in its concept, that is, considered in its truth, not merely the simple; but, as *abstract*, it is already *posited* as infected with *negation*".

2. *External* reflexion has a different way of setting forth the relation between Being and Naught, and, as we should expect, it is a very shallow and superficial way. Pure reflexion is the immediate act of the infant logic; external reflexion is the self-confident, but trivial, worthless act of the youthful logic, which knows only the outside appearance of things, but thinks it "knows it all". Being an act of comparison, external reflexion must have some objects given to it, and is merely concerned with the resemblance or the difference of these objects as they appear to the subject who reflects only upon the surface of them. In the present instance, before external reflexion can act, it must have both Being and Naught come before it, and then it must compare them. These conditions are met in Hegel's treatment of these categories in the text of his *Greater Logic*, where he says: "*Being, pure Being*—without any further determination. In its undetermined immediacy, it is only like itself nor is it unlike anything else; it has no difference within itself, nor any as against what is without. If any determination or contents were distinguished within it, or were made the means of setting it down as distinct from something else, it would not be maintained in its purity. It is pure indeterminateness and vacuity. There is *nothing* to be perceived in it, if we can here speak of perceiving; or rather it is only this pure, empty perceiving itself. Just as little is anything to be thought in it: or rather it is likewise only this empty

---

[1] I., 94 (100).

[2] I., 73 (78): "Es ist nichts in ihm anzuschauen". But see below.

[3] P. 65 above.

thought. Being, the undetermined immediate, is in fact *Naught,* and nothing more or less than Naught." [1]

Here we see that after Hegel has defined Being, he tells us that in this category we see *nothing.* This may be taken to mean one of two things. One meaning may be that which we have already indicated in discussing the point of view of pure reflexion : [2] "In the thought that thinks the category of pure Being, we perceive besides the category of Naught". If this were the correct paraphrase we should expect "Nichts" and not "nichts," for elsewhere Hegel always capitalises his categories; here both in the edition of 1812 and in the two issues of the second edition, the word is not capitalised. We may conclude that this is not the meaning of the passage, and we are then forced to the alternative that Hegel's thought is this : "In such an undetermined perception or thought as we have in pure Being, there is *not anything* to be seen or thought. Indeed we have a mere *objectless* perception or thought ; and just such a *lack* of object for perception or thought is what we mean by *Naught.* Hence the category of undetermined Being is, in fact, exactly the category of undetermined Naught, no more, no less."

If this is the line of thought, as it seems to be, it is clear that Hegel could never have said that the category of pure Being, so defined, was the category of pure Naught, unless the latter category with its meaning were already *independently* in his mind, waiting to be compared with the former. For Hegel has just said that *of itself pure Being has no resemblances.* The recognition, therefore, of any likeness to something else, or of any identity with something else, cannot have been forced upon him by the category itself that is now the object of thought ; but it must be the result of an external reflexion on his part, seeing that external reflexion differs from the internal reflexion of the absolute method just in this, that it does not obtain its result by a process that the *object* of thought performs. But if the identification of Being and Naught has been accomplished by external reflexion, then the category of Naught does not arise dialectically out of the category of Being, but is merely pronounced identical with that category by an external arbiter who decides nothing on its intrinsic merits.

That the course of thought in this passage is that of external reflexion is further shown in the next paragraph, where Hegel proceeds to justify the identification of Being and Naught by rehearsing fully the definition of Naught, and by

---

[1] I., 72 and 73 (77 and 78).   [2] P. 67 above.

showing that it is exactly the same as that of pure Being. "*Naught, pure Naught;* it is simple likeness to self, complete vacuity, absence of determinateness and contents, lack of distinctions within itself. In so far as perception or thought may be here mentioned, it is generally considered a distinction whether something or *nothing* be perceived or thought. To perceive or to think nothing, therefore, has a meaning; the two" (*i.e.*, something and nothing) " are distinct; hence Naught *is* (exists) in our perception or thought; or rather it is empty perception and thought itself, and is the same empty perception or thought as pure Being. Naught is therefore the same determination, or rather lack of determination, and hence altogether the same thing, that pure Being is."[1] Here it is evident that Hegel is merely comparing, point by point, the two categories, and as a result pronounces a judgment of identity between them. In short, *he is simply engaging in external reflexion.* But besides identifying the two categories, he also remarks upon a *distinction* which is commonly held to exist between the no categories. It must, however, be noticed that he here offers proof of the validity of this distinction. He merely appeals to current opinion; such an appeal surely is not a dialectical process.

It seems to me that one cannot escape the conviction that in the two paragraphs we have here examined, the procedure is one of external reflexion, and not a dialectical procedure by internal reflexion. To repeat what has been said, comparison of two categories, which of themselves do not prompt to any such comparison, leads the author to say that they are identical; current opinion as to their distinctness leads him to animadvert upon this distinction. It should be observed, however, that from such an identity as has been established, he has no right to say that Being and Naught are unseparated and inseparable, and that each vanishes in the other, and that the truth is neither the one nor the other, but the effected transition of the one into the other, all of which he does say in the following paragraph—he has no right to say this, unless he merely means that the psychological association in the thinker's mind between Naught and the definition of Being, and between Being and the definition of Naught, is so strong that, when he thinks of the definition of Being, the thought of Naught arises inevitably by spontaneous associative processes, and *vice versâ*.

The conclusion of this examination, therefore, is that in

I., 73 (78).

Hegel's *Greater Logic* the whole of the text that treats of the categories, Being and Naught, so far as the identification and the distinction of the two categories go, is concerned with exhibiting the work of external reflexion. Now the question arises, whether these paragraphs contain the only representation given by Hegel of the relation between these categories. If so, his case is hopeless. He is unmistakably convicted of using in the dialectic an instrument that he has in the most explicit terms declared to be unavailable for the purpose; and the unity that is brought about between Being and Naught is as blank a self-identity as was either pure Being or pure Naught. *There is no movement.* His thought is as changeless as the Brahman's, who " year in and year out gazes at the tip of his own nose and mutters ' Om, Om, Om ' to himself or else keeps silent ".[1] But did Hegel mean to palm off this paralysis of thought, this movelessness of external reflexion, as a genuine dialectical movement of vital inner reflexion? Are we forced to the alternative of saying, either that he himself was deceived in the matter, or else that he tried to deceive others? Surely not, when in the very first paragraph of his first remark[2] on this passage he tells us that in pure Naught he is conceiving *only the abstract negation,* and of course we may conclude from the distinction he is constantly making between abstract negation and dialectical negation that he is *not* dealing with the latter. Indeed, he tells us expressly that his purpose is not " to deal with the form of the opposition" (between Being and Naught) " that is, at the same time, with the form of the *relation* between them, but with abstract, immediate negation, with Naught purely independent, with unrelated denial—which, if one would, one could express by bare *not* ". If it had been his purpose to exhibit the second category in its *dialectical* form and in its dialectical relation, it would have been proper to substitute Non-Being for Naught, and in such a category all the dialectical characteristics of the negative would have manifested themselves. "For in *Non-Being* the relation to *Being* is contained ; it is both Being and the negation of Being expressed in *one* word ; Naught, as it is in Becoming." He thus disavows, in as clear and unmistakable terms as language can provide, any attempt to exhibit a dialectical movement in what he has said about the identity and about the distinctness of Being and Naught, when treating those categories in their purity.

[1] I., 92 (97).   [2] I., 74 (79).

THE DIALECTICAL METHOD. (II.)

[*Off-printed from* MIND : *a Quarterly Review of Psychology and Philosophy*. *Vol. VII., N.S., No. 26.*]

BY PROF. E. B. McGILVARY.

RETURNING now from the remarks to the text of the work, with the third paragraph of the first chapter[1] we enter upon a new movement of thought altogether. The identity of Being and Naught is still maintained and also their distinction ; but this identity and this distinction are no longer the identity and the distinction of *indifferent* objects which have been compared by an indifferent manipulator. Their identity becomes the unity of an organic whole in which their distinction is merely the variety of the organic factors entering into such a whole, a variety that is not, and cannot be, subjected to such a tension that a *separation* between the factors takes place. The dialectic engine has, up to this point, been revolving upon a turn-table operated by external force ; from now on, it makes its way forward by its own power.

3. This remark leads us to our next task, which is to consider the relation that *inner* reflexion establishes between Being and Naught, and to see how Hegel exhibits this relation. But here we are likely to be called to a halt. We shall be told that Hegel nowhere indicates such a relation for us. And such an eminent authority on the Hegelian dialectic as Dr. W. T. Harris may be cited as conceding the truth of this contention ; and, indeed, Dr. Harris does say that Hegel throws no light on the subject. The dialectic here takes a "hidden step," the logical chain contains a "suppressed link".[2] He thinks that Hegel himself knew well enough what the relation is, but he knew it so well that he did not think it possible that any one else could be ignorant of it ; hence he has not touched upon the subject directly at all ; and the expositor must "undertake a new analysis with a view to discover if possible that hidden step ". That, if the

[1] I., 78 (78).

[2] *Hegel's Logic : A Book on the Genesis of the Categories of the Mind. A Critical Exposition.* By William T. Harris, LL.D., U.S. Commissioner of Education. Chicago : S. C. Griggs & Company, 1890. P. 172.

need existed, Dr. Harris has supplied it, I do not question, and that Dr. Harris has shown the nature of this step in a far more lucid exposition than it was Hegel's good fortune to hit upon, I do not question. What I do question is that Hegel is silent as to the true dialectical process here.

The paragraph in which he treats of Becoming expresses the dialectical relation between Being and Naught. It is true that it is couched in the most distinctively Hegelian diction, whereas Dr. Harris writes in a language which he who runs may read. A literal translation of the Hegelian dialect of the passage I refer to runs thus : " *Pure Being and pure Naught are thus the same.* The truth, however, is neither Being nor Naught, but the fact that Being—not makes, but —*has made* a transition into Naught, and Naught into Being. But just as certainly is the truth not their indistinguishableness, but the fact that *they are not the same,* that they are *absolutely distinct,* yet also unseparated and inseparable; and that *each* vanishes immediately *in its opposite.* Their truth is, thus, this *movement* of the immediate vanishing of the one in the other—is, namely, *Becoming ;* a movement in which both are distinct, but with a distinction which is immediately just as certainly cancelled." [1]

What Hegel means by the " *truth* " of any category is that in which alone it has any being, that in which it functions as a moment,. but apart from which, in independence of which, it has. .o reality at all. And what he means by the vanishing of a category in its opposite, is the loss of it as an *independent* category in the engulfing organic totality of its dialectical negative. But the category that thus loses its life finds it again in the fuller life of the higher category into which it has been translated. If, then, the truth of Being and Naught is Becoming, " we see, therefore," to use Dr. Harris' words, " that we really thought a Becoming instead of an isolated term which we have named Being or Naught ".[2]

Dr. Harris would perhaps say to this, that he does not deny that Hegel states accurately enough the *result* of the process in this case ; what he denies is that he depicts the *process itself in the very act.* Hegel shows *that* the result is thus and so, but not *why* it is thus and so. And it is this explanation that Dr. Harris proceeds to give, and which I may summarise by saying that *pure* Being cannot be thought, and that for two reasons : first, to think Being as pure or indeterminate is to *determine* it by its contrast with all determined

---

[1] L., 73 and 74 (78 and 79).   [2] *Op. cit.,* p. 173.

independent actuality '.[1] Not only is the transition now necessary to the categories, but the transition *is* the categories. The reality in any finite category, in this stage, consists only in its summing up those which went before, and in leading on to those which come after." [2]

Now, before we can satisfactorily enter upon a discussion of this point, it will be necessary to make some preliminary remarks about the *double aspect* in which the categories appear in the *Logic*. The primary purpose of the *Logic* is to show how even the most abstract and seemingly independent and inorganic category contains within itself the life of the whole system of all-inclusive Thought; and how this life, if allowed full play, will develop that barren category through all the stages of thought up to the highest. Now, as this category grows under our observation, we see it taking the form of other categories familiar to us. Thus in the very development of the lowest category we reach other categories whose evolution it is the business of logic to display. Hence it is not necessary to give a separate genealogical table to each category; but the pedigree of one category will be the pedigree of many—but, from one point of view,[3] *not the pedigree of all*. And this is an important point. There are categories that, in the form in which we ordinarily use them, or rather in which we *think* we use them, are not to be found in the direct line of march from pure Being towards the goal of the Absolute Idea. But though not on the line of march, they are near by, and it takes only a little flank movement to sweep them into it. But this flank movement arrests the procession "for the subjective spirit," as Hegel would say. It *appears as if* there were a zigzag movement with constant stops, and not a "never-halting march".[4]

I may illustrate what I mean by borrowing and developing the metaphor Hegel uses for representing the absolute unity of thought. This unity is a circle; thought's movement is in an orbit that returns upon itself. But suppose that one has not yet discovered the orbit, does not even know whether there be any orbit or any movement; suppose one loses one's perspective, and, from any position, views two points in the circumference of the circle. These points

---

[1] "*Enc.*, Section 159."

[2] *Op. cit.*, pp. 123, 124.

[3] I wish to call especial attention to this reservation. For, from another point of view, it *is* the pedigree of all.

[4] I., 89 (41): "In unaufhaltsamem . . . Gange".

may appear to him *side by side*, rather than *one in advance of the other*. The more advanced point is then viewed as if it were collateral with the nearer; hence when a movement is discovered and is supposed to be in a bee-line from the point of observation through one of these points on to the infinite, it will seem as though a digression must be made from this line in order to catch the other point into the movement. In the same way a higher category is viewed as if it were co-ordinate with a lower one; so viewed, it will not have all the characteristics it should have, else it would not appear co-ordinate. In such a case, it is clear that when the lower category has advanced to the higher, it will not have passed through the form the higher takes *when reduced to a lower plane*. Now, as ordinary thought is abstract and thinks its categories in their abstractness, and not in their concreteness, it will be necessary, when dialectic comes alongside of a category in its abstract form, to show how this abstract category develops itself into the same concrete fulness into which its seeming co-ordinate was developed. To change the figure, the stone which, in the structure of speculative logic, has its significance only as resting on the lower stones and furnishing a basis for the higher, is by the common thinker torn out of its place and used as an independent unit. It is the business of the speculative builder, when he reaches this stone in its structural place, to show that even when lying apart it bears traces upon itself that cannot fail to indicate that such isolation is not proper to it, but that it belongs to an architectural system; and to show that these traces also indicate *where* it belongs in that system.

But even this is not all. Common understanding has its own ways of artificially grouping these abstract categories. One way, and a very favourite way, especially in dealing with the categories that dialectic reaches first, is to pair them off, and to set each member of a pair over against the other, as of equal rank, but mutually incompatible. Thus from the abstract point of view, these paired-off categories are contradictory to each other; and what dialectic does, appears to be a reconciling of these contradictions. When Hegel, therefore, speaks of any category "as such," he means that category regarded as the "unspeculative" thinker regards it; that is, as leading to no dialectical result, and even as independent of the process by which speculative logic has reached it. And when he speaks of its "opposite," he means, in the lower categories, what the abstract thinker regards as its irreconcilable contradictory; and when he speaks of "reconciling" these contradictories, he is merely using language that repre-

But to say that Being arose *historically* by the generative act of Naught is very different from saying that when once born into history it has a *logical* bond binding it to its psychological parent. The logician must examine the category itself, in order to discover its relationship; the testimony of genealogical tables is external testimony. Family marks are worth more than family Bibles. The logician who investigates his category finds that it is *essentially* Naught—not the abstract Naught of the unreflecting consciousness, but the Naught that is a synthetic unity of Being and its opposite, the Naught that is Becoming.[1] But when he is *just* beginning his investigation, he has not yet made the discovery.[2] He merely sees Being and Naught side by side. There does not seem to be an *advance* from Being to Naught; Naught seems to have been reached *already*, when Being is reached. He seems to have two immediate data. But after his investigations have progressed somewhat, he sees that, when he had what appeared to be two data, he really had one concrete category, to the two moments of which he paid attention separately. Being stands side by side with Naught, because neither is pure, because each is merely an organic element in Non-Being, the concrete negation of Being. It is because Being is *what* it is *only* in that which robs it of its abstract independence, in that which negates it and thus posits it—it is because of this, that Being passes into Naught. But when the logician sees this, he also sees that this Naught into which Being passes is a *dialectical* negative, and *not* an *abstract* negative. But as the dialectical negative is richer than its positive, the passing from Being to Naught is an *advance* in a straight line, not a transverse motion. To sum this up in an expression which reproduces almost *verbatim* an expression of Hegel's, Naught appears immediately in Being just because Being is Being, *only* in the higher unity of Naught; just because Being is Being, *only* as an essential moment in the concrete totality of its negative.

The logician is a spectator of a performance by Hermann, the magician, and must not go behind the scenes. He is to let the magical feats begin where it is the good will of the magician to let them begin, and he must await developments. All he can do is to register the fact that when Being appears

---

[1] What I say here and in the whole of this paragraph, as to the identity of the antithesis and synthesis when they are viewed dialectically, will be justified in the sequel.

[2] That is, unless he has mastered the *presupposition* of logic. See the *Philosophical Review*, September, 1897, p. 497 ff.

behind the lights, Naught stands by her side ; or to be more exact in the metaphor, he notes that Being appears Protean ; now she is Being and now she is Naught. He cannot see this metamorphosis going on ; but he knows that it *has* taken place ; for when he thinks that he is looking at Being, he discovers that he is really looking at Naught. He must wait patiently, and keep his eyes open and his wits alert. By-and-by he will detect the secret of the illusion. And he will then have the satisfaction of knowing that he comes by the solution of the puzzle without committing a breach of propriety. He has not sacrificed his dignity as a logician by peeping into psychological dressing-rooms.

Two questions now arise. (1) If Hegel really knew the true dialectical nature of the relation between Being and Naught, why did he not express it clearly in the text of his work when treating of these first two categories, instead of reserving the statement for his treatment of the third category and for the remarks? (2) Is not Hegel's way of stating this dialectical relation a *petitio principii* ?

(1) The answer to the first question can be given only when we go back to what has been said in another place about the *double* aspect of many categories.[1] Pure Being has this double aspect. Regarded *abstractly*, you have a category that can be treated only by external reflexion, because such a category is not dialectical ; just as a hand, regarded *geometrically*, cannot be treated *biologically*. We set a restriction upon the scope of our investigation, and cannot go beyond the restriction until we remove it.

Regarded in another way, Being is not an abstract identity, but is only a moment in a higher synthesis. This is the true dialectical way of regarding it ; and the logician, if he has mastered the presupposition of his science, is conscious that this is the only dialectical way of looking at it. He knows that the category of thought-thinking-self, or pure Being, is not a category of dead self-identity. He knows that *thought is thinking* this category, and that therefore this category is only a distinction, a moment, within thought. It is an organic member within an organism. Hence it is pure Being, not as *abstract*, but as determined by its *own* nature of being organically related with its fellow-categories.

A careful reader of Hegel will therefore see that in A and B, on pages 72 (77) and 73 (78) of the first volume of the *Greater Logic*, the author is treating two categories by

---

[1] See January number of MIND, p. 57 ff.

external reflexion; in C, he is treating them as they stand organically interrelated within a higher unity. In A and B, he is showing to ordinary consciousness the contradiction into which it falls, when it uses Being and Naught as it is constantly using them. And as the demonstration is for the sake of ordinary consciousness, it must be conducted in the only way which ordinary consciousness can follow, the way of external reflexion. Having thus shown the impossibility of the abstractly pure Being and pure Naught of ordinary consciousness, by showing how in their abstraction they are *absolutely identical*, and how their distinction is only a make-believe, Hegel then proceeds in C to state the *truth* with regard to them. This truth is that they have an identity in a higher unity, in which they also maintain their distinctness. In the independent character in which they *purport* to exist, they do not exist. They exist only as *moments*, only as *distinctions*.[1] This thought is very clearly brought out in C, and is expanded in the latter part of the

---

[1] Since writing the text I have read Mr. Hobhouse's discussion of the dialectical movement in his most valuable volume, *The Theory of Knowledge*, pp. 197-202. Does it bewray a heart too wickedly Hegelian in its desire to sublate everything in sight, when I say that I admit the truth contained in his characterisation of the Hegelian method, only I do not think it is the whole truth? Is it a case in which "Hegelism benignantly smiles at" her opponents' "exertions, and murmurs, 'If the red slayer thinks he slays'; 'When me they fly, I am the wings,' etc."? (Professor James' *The Will to Believe*, p. 293). Mr. Hobhouse says that "the dialectical process belongs to the pathology of thought". If what I maintained in the January number of MIND (p. 57 ff.) be true, then one aspect—but not the most important nor the most dialectical aspect —of dialectic does concern "the pathology of thought". But even supposing that this were an exhaustive account of the matter, is healthy thought on such a subject as the real function and value of abstraction so common, and is unsound thought so rare, that Hegel's attempt to supply a therapeutic is to be patronisingly judged as having indeed " a justification and a value of its own," but as being for all that mighty "tedious"? Again, when Mr. Hobhouse says that "this process . . . is set on foot, not by abstraction as such, but by the one-sided use of abstraction," does he not know that it is just this one-sided use of abstraction and *only* this that Hegel calls abstraction? The kind of abstract which Mr. Hobhouse rightly recognises as "a genuine characteristic of reality," Hegel recognises as such also. He sins merely by calling it not an "abstract," but a "distinction," a "moment," etc. Is it quite fair then in Mr. Hobhouse to hold Hegel up to general condemnation for *one-sidedness*, merely because Hegel was not lucky enough to anticipate Mr. Hobhouse's terminology? This seems to me to be but another of the innumerable instances in which an Hegelian insight gets itself "tricked and flounced " in some *fin de siècle* garb and then goes before the bar of public opinion as a witness to prove the philosophic barrenness of Hegel's mind, because forsooth it did not bring forth this offspring *ready-clad* in the most modern fashion.

second remark;[1] but it is unnecessary to quote the passage here.

Let us state this turn of thought in another way. We must begin our logical movement with pure Being. But pure Being has a double aspect. It may be regarded as an unrelated abstract, or it may be regarded as merely an organic factor in a thought-unity. We begin with the first aspect of it, and find that it is a *false* aspect. We then take it in its other aspect ; but we now find that really we are dealing as much with the organic unity to which it belongs as with the factor that belongs to this unity. That is, we may say that on this showing we really do not begin with pure Being, but with *Becoming*, which has Being as its moment. But such a statement must not be read with too much emphasis on the negative side of it ; for as we now begin with Becoming, which has Being and Naught as its moments, the logical beginning, as Hegel defines it, is not Becoming, but the moments of Becoming. Becoming, being a concrete category analysable into Being and Naught, cannot be the logical beginning in this sense, but its *elements* are logically prior to it; and Being is the element with which we must begin. But this Being is no longer pure Being *as abstract*, but Being *as a moment in Becoming*. But in saying this we are already saying that in one sense we begin with Becoming. A little further reflexion will show that there is no contradiction in these two statements. There are two kinds of logical presuppositions, and therefore two logical beginnings. There is the presupposition on the part of the organic unity; for it presupposes its distinctions ; hence logical movement must begin with these distinctions. But they are distinctions, only on the presupposition of a unity within which they have their being ; hence logical movement must begin with the unity. Hegel, in saying that the initial category must be without presuppositions, means that it must be the *ultimate distinction*. In saying that Being presupposes absolute knowledge, absolute thought, he means that this ultimate distinction has in its turn factors, and thus becomes the *ultimate unity* in which what was just now the organic whole is a distinction ; therefore the ultimate distinction is *not* ultimate, in the sense of being unanalysable.[2]

To apply all this to the case in point, and to sum up the whole discussion in an answer to the question we started to

---

[1] I., 85 and 86 (91).

[2] A fuller discussion of this reciprocity will follow in a continuation of this article in a subsequent number of MIND.

answer : Hegel *does* represent the inner dialectical movement in the *text* of his *Logic ;* but does not begin to do so till he comes to Becoming ; because it is only after he has Becoming, that he has Being as its moment. But this " after " is also a " before," but not a " before " that is not also an " after ". Hence, because pure abstract Being and pure abstract Naught are " befores " that are *not also* " afters," he begins with them only to show that he *cannot* begin with them. He does not really begin until he gets to Becoming, for it is only *then* that he has something prior to Becoming. These paradoxes may perhaps do something toward reducing to order the confusion that has flourished so long over this whole realm under the reign of the critics.

(2) The answer to this question leads us naturally to the second question asked above.[1] At first sight this question seems a poser. For it appears as if the logical validity of the final result of the logical process depended on the logical validity of the movement in the first triad, and yet the logical validity of this movement appears to be assured to us only by the final result. Is not this a *petitio ?* Now, there is no question that there is a circular movement in this reasoning. Hegel himself admits it : " By this advance, then, the beginning loses the one-sidedness it had in being altogether an immediate and abstract category. It becomes something mediated, and the line of progressive movement in this science thus becomes a *circle*. At the same time, it follows that what constitutes the beginning is, in the beginning, not yet truly known, since at this stage it is as yet undeveloped and is without contents. It also follows that it is only the logical science, and that, too, in its completed development, that affords us a perfect knowledge of the beginning, a knowledge full of contents and truly grounded." [2]

But the circle is not a *vicious* circle. We do not begin with some *arbitrarily assumed* premiss. We begin where the nature of our task requires us to begin. This task is, as already stated, to show how even the lowest category leads irresistibly on to the highest. We start, therefore, with what is apparently the lowest, namely, pure Being. Inevitably, we know not as yet how or why Naught emerges before our view, and so identifies itself with Being that the two are inseparable. From this indissoluble but as yet mysterious union, into which our first category spontaneously enters, the progress is understood, and is seen to be logically necessary and perfectly uniform to the very last ; and then,

---

[1] See page 238, above.　　　[2] I., 61 (65 and 66).

behold, we reach the point from which we set out at the beginning,—but with this difference, that, whereas at first we did not seem to know anything about this category, not even why it was inseparably connected with another, now we know all about it; and among other things, we now know why it led to the second category, and we see that its relation to the second is exactly the relation of the first category of every triad to its *dialectical* antithesis, as will appear in the sequel.   Thus we step upon a platform that appears to be stationary ; but to our great surprise we find that it moves, we know not why.   Subsequently the movement of the platform brings us within sight of the propelling machinery.   The movement continues, and finally we are back where we started.   But now we know the reason for the movement that was at first so inexplicable.[1]

[1] We should remember, however, that this inexplicability is only a psychological ἀπορία.   The logical has no embarrassments.   There is nothing *now* hidden from it, that shall *subsequently* be made known.   The logician, as *a man enacting a history in time,* meets with many perplexities and many overwhelming surprises in his studies *at* logic.   The logician, *as a logician,* is surprised at no truth that he sees in his studies *in* logic.   He *eternally* knows it ; otherwise I do not see how he could ever *come* to know it in any year of grace.   To say the same thing in other words, the student who has mastered the presupposition of his logical science knows that his first dialectical category is an organic member in an all-inclusive totality of thought.   He therefore knows why his first category leads to the second.   The transition is for him a *moveless* movement, a *timeless* process, of inner reflexion.   But for a student who begins with a *mere resolve* to consider thought as such, the transition is a great mystery, only to be revealed in the fulness of time.   At some moment in his student's career, there will dawn upon him the light which eternally lighteth every man.

(*To be concluded.*)

THE DIALECTICAL METHOD. (III.)

(*Conclusion.*)

[*Off-printed from* MIND : *a Quarterly Review of Psychology and
Philosophy. Vol. VII., N.S., No. 27.*]

By Prof. E. B. McGilvary.

II. Let us now address ourselves to the contention that
there is another kind of change in the method of the dialectic, a change from dependence upon contradiction into absolute indifference to contradiction. Mr. McTaggart says that
the difference is greatest between the method employed at
the very beginning of the process and the method employed
at its end. In the categories of Being, neither the thesis nor
the antithesis " is in any respect more advanced than the
other, and neither of them can be said to be more closely
connected than the other with the synthesis, in which both
of them alike find their explanation and reconciliation. But
when we come to Essence the matter is changed. Here the
transition from thesis to antithesis is still indeed from positive to negative, but it is more than merely this. The antithesis is not merely complementary to the thesis, but is a ·
correction of it. It is consequently more concrete and true
than the thesis, and represents a real advance. And the
transition to the synthesis is not now made so much from
the comparison of the other two terms as from the antithesis
alone. For the antithesis does not now merely oppose a
contrary defect to the original defect of the thesis. It cor-
rects, to some degree, that original mistake, and therefore has
—to use the Hegelian phraseology—' the truth ' of the thesis
more or less within itself. As the action of the synthesis is
to reconcile the thesis and the antithesis it can only be de-
duced from the comparison of the two. But if the antithesis
has—as it has in Essence—the thesis as part of its own significance, it will present the whole of the data which the
synthesis requires, and it will not be necessary to recur to the
thesis, before the step to the synthesis is taken.

" But although the reconciliation can be inferred from the
second term, apart from the first, a reconciliation is still
necessary. For, while the antithesis is an advance upon the
thesis, it is also opposed to it. It is not simply a completion

of it, but also a denial, though a denial which is already an approximation to union. This element of opposition and negation tends to disappear in the categories of the Notion. As these approach the end of the whole process, the steps are indeed discriminated from one another, but they can scarcely be said to be in opposition. For we have now arrived at a consciousness more or less explicit that in each category all that have gone before are summed up, and all that are to come after are contained implicitly. ' The movement of the Notion is after all to be looked on only as a kind of play. The other which it sets up is in reality not another.' And, as a consequence, the third term merely completes the second without correcting one-sidedness in it, in the same way as the second term merely expands and completes the first. As this type is realised, in fact, the distinctions of the three terms gradually lose their meaning. There is no longer an opposition produced between two terms and mediated by a third. Each term is a direct advance on the other before it. The object of the process is not now to make the one-sided complete, but the implicit explicit. For we have reached a stage when each side carries in it already more or less consciousness of that unity of the whole which is the synthesis, and requires development rather than refutation." [1]

A few pages farther on, we read : " We may draw several important conclusions with regard to the general nature of the dialectic, from the manner in which the form changes as it advances towards completion. The first of these is one which we may fairly attribute to Hegel himself, since it is evident from the way in which he deals with the categories, although it is not explicitly noticed by him. This is the subordinate place held by negation in the whole process. We have already observed that the importance of the negation in the dialectic is by no means primary. In the first place Hegel's Logic is very far from resting, as is supposed by some critics, on the violation of the law of contradiction. It rather rests on the impossibility of violating that law, and on the necessity of finding, for every contradiction, a reconciliation in which it vanishes. And not only is the idea of negation destined always to vanish in the synthesis, but even its temporary introduction is an accident, though an inevitable accident. . . . But this can now be carried still further. Not only is the presence of negation in the dialectic a mere accident, though a necessary one, of the gradual

[1] *Op. cit.*, pp. 124, 125.

completion of the idea. We are now led to consider it as an accident which is necessary indeed in the lower stages of the dialectic, but which is gradually eliminated in proportion as we proceed further." [1]

I have quoted thus largely in order that the issue may be clearly defined. My aim is not so much to controvert the expositor, but to expound his author and mine. But here, as in so many other instances, exposition is most effectively accomplished by a refutation of a counter-exposition. As every affirmation is also a negation, it is often well that what one denies should be brought clearly before consciousness, in order that what one affirms may be the more significant. As I understand Hegel, he affirms exactly what his commentator denies; and to understand the affirmation, it is well to understand the denial also.

It is my purpose to prove that in respect of the relation in opposition between the thesis and the antithesis, and in respect of the dialectical efficiency of the negative, there is really no change in Hegel's Logic from the very first triad to the very last. In order to do this, I shall attack the problem of the method of the initial triad, believing that a complete exhibition of the method there employed will be in itself a complete refutation of Mr. McTaggart's position.

As we enter upon this problem, we must recall what has been said about the double character of some of the categories, and about the so-called reconciliation of contradictories. [2] The true view of the movement, even in the categories of Being, is that the true dialectical negative of any thesis is not the abstract antithesis of that thesis, but it is the so-called synthesis of that thesis with the abstract antithesis; so that, if we are going to count steps, we may say that in one very important sense the dialectical movement is not triadic, [3] although, of course, if we consider the two aspects of the negative as two distinct steps in the process; that is, if we consider as one step the viewing of the negative as abstractly negative and as another step the viewing of it as concretely positive, we do have a triadic movement. But this whole matter of counting steps is a senseless procedure, an external reflexion; and the witticisms based upon it only show the shallowness of the views of the wits.

---

[1] *Op. cit.*, p. 134.   [2] See January number of MIND, pp. 57-60.

[3] See III., 333, 334 (343-344), where Hegel shows that the movement may be considered tetradic or dyadic as well as triadic; but all such enumeration is "superficial and external".

Hegel's own testimony on this point is decisive. "It" (*i.e.*, the negation of any concept) "is a new concept, but one higher and richer than the preceding; for it has become richer by the negation or opposite of that concept. It thus contains its predecessor and more too, and is the unity of ∨that predecessor and its opposite."[1] This is what he says in the Introduction to the *Greater Logic*. He says the same thing at the very end of this work,[2] where, having traversed the long road that leads from pure Being to the Absolute Idea, he reviews the course that has been accomplished, and pays particular attention to the method that has achieved the result. There he devotes some eight or ten pages to the full treatment of the relation between thesis, antithesis, and synthesis, or, as he there calls them, "the first," "the second," and "the third"; and he looks at this relation from many points of view. I cannot quote the whole passage, although any one who wishes to understand the method thoroughly should make himself perfectly familiar with what is there said. All I can do here is to quote in part : "The second" (*i.e.*, the antithesis), "which has thus arisen, is accordingly the negative of the first ; and, to take anticipatory account of what follows, it is the first negative. The immediate" (*i.e.*, the thesis) "has, on this negative side, perished in its other ; but that other is essentially not the empty negative, Naught, which is taken for the usual result of dialectic ; but it is the other of the first, the negative of the immediate.[3] Thus it is determined as the *mediate*—in short, contains within itself the determination of the first" (*i.e.*, of the thesis). "The first is hence essentially *preserved* and *kept* in its other. To keep fast hold of the positive in its own negative, in the content of the presupposition, in the result—this is the most important thing in the knowledge that belongs to the stage of reason. . . . What is, accordingly, now present is the mediated, which at first, or when likewise taken immediately, is also a simple category; for since the first has perished in it, only the second is present. Now, because the first is also contained in the second, and the second is the truth of the first, this unity can be expressed as a proposition, in which the immediate is put as subject, and the mediate as its predicate. . . . The second category, the negative or mediate, is, further, likewise the *mediating* category. At first it can be taken as a

---

[1] I., 39 (41).   [2] III., 328 (338), *seq.*

[3] The thought would be better expressed by the use of hyphens : "the other-of-the-first, the negative-of-the-immediate," and below, "the negative-of-the-positive".

simple category; but viewed as it is in its truth, it is a relation or an essential relation. For it is, indeed, the negative, but the negative of the positive, and includes the positive within itself. It is thus the other, not of something to which it is indifferent,—for then it would not be an other, nor would it be a relation or an essential relation,—but it is the other *by virtue of itself* (*an sich*), the *other-of-another*. Therefore it includes *its own* other in itself, and is, accordingly, as this contradiction, *the explicitly posited dialectic of its own self.* . . . The second, as contrasted with the first, is itself the determinate, *i.e.*, is distinction or essential relation. The dialectical moment in it consists, hence, in positing the unity that is contained in it. If, therefore, the negative, the determinate, *e.g.*, essential relation and judgment and all the categories that come under the second moment" (*i.e.*, appear as antithesis), "do not themselves, taken in their independence, already appear as contradiction and as dialectical, it is due to a mere defect of the thinking faculty, which does not bring its thoughts together. For the materials," adequate for the recognition of contradiction, "the opposite categories *in one relation*, are already explicitly posited, and present for thought. Formal thought, however, makes identity a law, and lets the contradictory content that it has before it be degraded into the sphere of presentative consciousness, into space and time; and there the contradictory is maintained in the reciprocal *externality* of coexistence or succession, and thus does not appear to consciousness to be in mutual contact. In its dealing with this content, formal thought lays down the definite principle that contradiction is not thinkable. In fact, however, the thinking of contradiction is the essential factor in conception. Even formal thought actually thinks contradiction; only, while thinking it, it refuses to recognise it, turns from it, and in that just-quoted principle betakes itself to abstract negation.

"The negativity just considered constitutes the critical point in the movement of the concept. It is the simple point of negative self-reference, the innermost fountain of all activity, of vital and spiritual self-movement, the dialectical soul that everything true has in it, and by which alone it is a truth."[1]

To bring out all the wealth of meaning that lies stored up in these cryptic utterances would take more pages than are at my disposal. But it requires no great space, and certainly no great penetration, to repeat some things that are

---

[1] III., 330-332 (340-342).

said by Hegel in the passage I have partly cited. The central thought of it all is this: *When we have reached any antithesis, we do not need to wait for a synthesis in order to reconcile that antithesis with its thesis; but the antithesis itself, viewed as speculative logic views it and not as abstract, make-believe, but impossible thought would view it, is already a synthesis of the thesis with the opposite of the thesis.*

In other words, the antithesis has two significations; or rather it may be regarded from two points of view. Looked at from one point of view, it is merely an abstract opposite of its thesis, having no *intimate* relation to it, living as a quarrelsome neighbour *beside* it, *separated* from it by an insurmountable wall of partition, through which only its objurgations can find passage. The law of identity keeps it bound down fast on its own side of the fence; the law of contradiction forbids its trespassing on its neighbour's premises; while the law of the excluded middle says that there is no fence between them. And thus this point of view opens before us a scene that is—illusion; "vanity of vanities, all is vanity". So we must betake ourselves to the other point of view, and see whether that will not display before us a substantive reality.

From this second point of view, the antithesis is no longer a virago living next door to the thesis, but is the indispensable, all-absorbing, husband-sublating wife, "the joy of its bosom, the plague of its life". The non-existent wall of separation no longer separates; it unites. The husband is seen to be only a member of a family, and the wife is the family.

But illustrations and all like aids to comprehension are only external. The matter must be understood in its native logical truth; and it seems to me that this truth is capable of being understood, and even of being expressed in language that is no more figurative than all languages must be. Let us try.

The negative of anything, as merely presentatively before consciousness (*als vorgestellt*), may appear to that consciousness with all suggestion of its intrinsic essential relation to its positive suppressed; only, one is tempted in such a case to appropriate Prof. James' happy word "sciousness," as a more faithful designation of such a mythical consciousness. When, for instance, I present to myself the image-idea of Naught, I may seem to have a mere vacuum as the only object before my consciousness, a vacuum which explicitly excludes the content of Being, and therefore has no Being in it. But this is a mere seeming. Because if it is a merely presented Naught and not a thought Naught, not a conceived Naught, then it is not Naught *to me*, and therefore the presentation of it to me is not consummated. The desired result is achieved only when I *think* what is proffered, as being Naught; and to think it as Naught is to think it as negative of Being, as Non-Being; that is, Being must be *present as rejected* within the thought that thinks Naught. I must think what-it-is-not, and think Naught as *not* what-it-is-not. Naught is, then, the synthesis, in thought, of Being and rejection or negation, a synthesis of elements which, if they could exist out of such synthesis, would be pure Being and pure denial or abstract pure Naught. It takes, thus, only a little psychological reflexion to see that the thought of the negative is, as a matter of fact, always a thought that includes its positive as a moment within it; and it takes but a little logical reflexion to see that it must be so. The thought of the negative is, therefore, not a dead self-identity, but is a *synthetic unity, with the positive that it negates as a distinction partly constitutive of it;* whereas the thought of the so-called positive is never achievable except as merely a part-thought within the organic whole of a negative thought. But such a negative thought is not merely negative; in denying the positive, it not only posits itself but it also posits as a factor within itself the positive which it itself denies.

Now, even when "common-sense" rises to the height from which it can see that the positive is only a part-thought, it makes the mistake of supposing that the negative is only another part-thought, along with which the positive part-thought makes a whole by external juxtaposition. It is perhaps Hegel's greatest merit to have seen the insufficiency and utter inadequacy of any such supposition, and to have made this his insight the instrument for the reconstruction of the science of logic, for the rescue of dialectic from the fate of being a mere capricious iconoclast, and for making it the constructive principle of philosophy, seeing that it was the constructive and not the destructive principle of thought. He saw that what is only positive does not exist, except as a merely apprehended but not yet comprehended member in a concrete whole; he saw that what is only negative does not exist except as a whole not recognised as a whole; and he saw that what in truth really exists, and what alone exists, is the negative whole of thought, which, because negative, has distinctions; which, because a whole, has the distinctions within it and not without; and which, because not negating something outside of it

or an independent other, is truly positive. As already
shown, this positive-negative whole, has, as its organic
constitutive factors, the positive and negation. The factors, regarded in themselves, in abstraction from the whole
in which alone they have being, are pure, *i.e.*, abstract
Being and abstract negativity or pure Naught. But so
regarded, they cannot be *thought*, and what cannot be thought
cannot be logical; and so long as they are not thought, they
have no dialectical character belonging to them. They get
dialectical character only when they are taken up into
thought; that is, when they cease to be mere unsubstantial
ghosts, mere make-believes which are not, and become real
thoughts that are. The dialectical movement is the change
from what they are not and never were and never could be,
but were supposed to be, to what they really are. Dialectic
is the nullifying of a nullity that parades itself in the guise
of an entity; but this nullity is not cancelled out of consideration. The abstractions that are shown by dialectic to
be nonentities are shown to be such, only in being shown to
be real organic factors in the one thing that can with any
propriety be called real, that is, in negative-positive thought,
or self-consciousness.

Now it is for the reason that the dialectical negative is
thus negative because what it negates is *within* it,—it is for
this reason that Hegel calls it "the other by virtue of itself,
the other-of-another" ("das Andere an sich selbst, das Andere
eines Andern"). It does not owe its otherness to the mere
accident of being arbitrarily and externally contrasted with
something to which it is indifferent, but it is an other because it has *in itself, as its own moment*, its other, by virtue of
which it has the characteristic of otherness. It is itself
the other-of-another, not what may be regarded as an other
—of something independent.

Having thus shown what is the true logical view of the
relation between the antithesis and the thesis, let us see
whether this relation does not hold in the very first triad.
As has already been shown, the first triad is not abstract
Being, abstract Naught, *and* Becoming. But it is Being
which has its reality *only in its negation;* which negation, *being
concrete*, is the synthetic unity of Being and its opposite,
Naught; in other words, that negation is Becoming. The
thought or category, Becoming, is just the same thought as
Non-Being when Non-Being is *thought*, and is not merely an
imaged abstraction. As Hegel says, "in Non-Being the
relation to Being is contained; it is both Being and the
negation of Being expressed in one word; Naught, as it

is in Becoming ".[1] Since it is thus a dialectical negative, which is richer than its thesis, including, as it does, both its thesis and the opposite of that thesis, it is "just as positive as it is negative"; and when thought of as positive we call it Becoming.

It would not be difficult to show that in any other so-called triad in the categories of Being, the antithesis, when thought, that is, when dialectical and not abstract, is already the synthesis. Take for instance the Finite, the false Infinite, and the true Infinite. The false Infinite is not really the antithesis in thought of the Finite; it is only by an unrealisable abstraction that the false Infinite has any being. To negate the Finite in thought one must think it as a moment in the Infinite; the Infinite cannot exclude it; hence the Infinite cannot be, in real thought, a false Infinite. And, again, the Finite cannot be thought except as a moment in the thought of the Infinite. Of course a finite thing may be discovered to consciousness by presentation without the presentation of the Infinite, for the Infinite cannot be presented at all. But this finite thing can be thought as finite, only as a distinction within a thought that thinks what the Finite is not, viz., the Infinite.

But this relation between thesis and synthetic antithesis in these early categories is exactly the relation that exists in the categories of Conception (*Begriff*). Let us take Concept, Judgment, Syllogism, as example of the later triads. A negation of what usually passes for a concept is a judgment; that is, you cannot in thought negate such a concept without *ipso facto* judging. Nor can you ever judge without *ipso facto* negating such a concept. That is to say, unless the so-called subject and the so-called predicate are kept distinct, kept in the negative reciprocity of distinction, there is no judgment. But if this distinction is a *bare* negation, a mutual *exclusion*, there is no judgment either. The so-called subject and the so-called predicate are not in external juxtaposition. The true logical subject[2]—not the so-called logical subject—includes the predicate while denying it, that is, while distinguishing it from itself. As Mr. Bosanquet says, " Subject and Predicate in the actual judgment are really distinct, as a real identity from or in its differences ". " You cannot affirm *without introducing a distinction or reference* into the content of the affirmation ;

---

[1] I., 74 (79).

[2] The true logical subject in " synthetic judgments " is the all-inclusive unity of the distinctions named in the subject and predicate, and in " analytic judgments " it is the unity analysed.

and yet such distinction or reference, *being part of what is affirmed, and not a relation between what is affirmed and something else,* cannot, it would seem, be the essence of the affirmation." [1] The subject, the all-inclusive unity of distinctions, is the *negative* unity of these distinctions, not their dead identity. But because that negative is thus a mediating unity, in which the so-called subject and the so-called predicate of the " synthetic judgment " are brought together, it is the syllogism. To recapitulate, the negative of the concept, as explained above, is judgment ; this negative of the concept regarded as positive, because not negative of something external to it, is the syllogism. Now the reader who has followed this very brief exhibition of the dialectic of Concept, Judgment, and Syllogism, will see that the method is exactly the same as that employed in the triad, Being, Naught, and Becoming.

We can now see what becomes of Mr. McTaggart's contention that the negative is only a necessary accident in the dialectical process, tending to disappear in the higher categories. We may traverse this contention in two ways. We may say truly that negation, far from being a necessary accident in the dialectical process, never appears in it—*meaning here by negation what Mr. McTaggart means by it ;* for the dialectical process is never " from one extreme to another extreme equally one-sided ".[2] And we may also say that negation is not an accident tending to disappear, because it is the very life of the process, and appears in the fulness of its power only when it has brought all things under its feet, as the All-in-All of the Absolute Idea.

It happens that abstract understanding puts over against the thesis some other would-be category, now in the relation of contradictory opposition, now of contrary opposition, now of subcontrary opposition ; and what disappears in the higher categories is the particular definite way the abstract understanding has of relating a lower abstract antithesis with its thesis ; and what takes its place is some other particular way. But what is permanent through all such changes on the part of abstract understanding, is the one way that dialectic has of advancing by negation from a lower category to the higher, in which alone the lower has being. " That by which the Concept accomplishes its self-advancement is the aforesaid negative that it has in it. This constitutes the truly dialectical feature." [3]

---

[1] Bosanquet's *Logic,* I., 82. The italics are mine, to emphasise what is here pertinent.

[2] *Op. cit.,* p. 134.   [3] I., 40 (43).

What we have already said will throw light upon another vexed question that concerns the nature of the dialectic. Is its method analytic or synthetic ? Is the first category a box within which the others are all contained, or is it a grain of sand to which the others are added to make a heap ? If this second form of putting the question fairly represents what is meant by the first form, the answer must be that it is neither analytic nor synthetic ; for such analysis and synthesis are nothing but mere partition and aggregation. But if by analysis is meant the bringing to explicit consciousness (*Setzung*) of what a category is in itself (*an sich*), and if by synthesis is meant the enrichment of a category by another which is not an externally indifferent other, then the answer must be that the process is both analytic and synthetic. For in an organism, analysis and synthesis are not inverse processes, but are the same process. And by this I mean something different from what Mr Bradley and Mr. Bosanquet mean when they say that there is no analysis without synthesis, and no synthesis without analysis. For what they mean is that a thought-whole does not crumble to pieces under the operation of analysis, but that the act of analysis can be performed and the result of analysis can be recognised as an analysis, only when in the same act these analytic elements are ideally held together in the whole, from the ideal disintegration of which they have arisen ; and that an intellectual synthesis can take place and be recognised as synthesis, only when the synthetic result is not a homogeneous whole, but the distinctions unified are still kept distinct. All this is true *even in the ideal partition and aggregation of spaced objects conceived merely as mutually external.* Now what I mean by the co-operation, or rather by the identity, of analysis and synthesis is something very different from this. One cannot analyse the conception one has of any member in an organic whole without finding in that conception the conception of the other members and of the whole within which they are members ; and this gives the analytic character to the operation. But at the same time these other members are truly *others*, and the whole is more than the part ; and this gives the synthetic character to the operation.

Let us hear what the great dialectician himself says on this subject : " This is what Plato demanded of knowledge, that it should consider things in themselves, in their absoluteness ; that is, partly, in their universality ; but also, partly, that one should not stray away from them, and should comprehend them, not in their environments, instances, and

external contrasts, but that one should keep them alone
before one's thoughts and bring to consciousness what is
immanent in them.   The method of absolute knowledge is
in so far *analytic*.   The fact that this method finds the further
determination of its initial universal entirely in this universal
alone, is the absolute objectivity of the conception,—and
the method is the assurance of this objectivity.   It is, however, just as much *synthetic*, since its object, determined in
its immediacy as simple universal, shows itself as an *other*,
by the very determinateness which it has in its immediacy
and universality.   This relation to a different something—a
relation which constitutes the object in itself—is, however,
not the same thing as is meant by synthesis in finite knowledge.   Already by its quite as analytic character of being a
relation *within a conception*, it is thoroughly distinguished from
this latter synthetic procedure.   This moment of *original
self-diremption (des Urtheils)*—a moment as synthetic as it is
analytic—by which this initial universal obtains out of itself
its determination of being its own other, is to be called the
dialectical moment." [1]

Let me give an illustration of Hegel's meaning by using
what, at first, seems not to admit of serving as such.   What
is the relation of a plane triangle to the space outside of it?
Of course, if merely looked at, the triangle is seen to be outside of the space that is outside of it.   Considered as mutually external, neither can by analysis be derived from the
other.   But instead of merely looking at the triangle, *think it*,
that is, bring it under conception, and proceed to examine
logically the concept you have of it.   Logically, the concept
of it is the concept of a plane-figure-bounded-by-three-straight-
lines.   That is to say, we find as an element held logically
within the organic unity of the concept "triangle," the concept "line".   Now examine this concept "line"—again
avoid merely looking at it in a passive gaze—and you will
find that it is the concept of limit-between-two-surfaces.
That is, the concept "surface" is an element held logically
within the organic unity of the concept "line".   Again,
examining this concept "surface," you will find that it is the
concept of limit-between-two-solids ; so that, here again, we
find that the concept "solid" is included as an element
logically within the concept "surface".   Thus we find that
the tridimensional space, circumjacent to a plane triangle, is
an *analytic element* in the very concept of that triangle.   But
it is no less true that this tridimensional space is the *inclusive*

[1] III., 326 (335-336).

concept, in which the concept of the triangle in its turn is an element ; that is, this tridimensonial space, when thought, is *synthetically* related to the triangle, having the triangle as an analytic element within it. We do not, and cannot, think tridimensional space as an element in a quadridimensional space. We think it as a moment in the concept of one or more of its dimensions, and think it as the total concept including its dimensions as its moments. The analysis of the concept of a dimension gives tridimensional space as a distinction within it, but this distinction is at the same time the synthesis of this dimension with the other dimensions. But such synthesis and such analysis are not juxtaposition of mutually external pieces and partition into mutually external segments. The analysis is the recognition of the distinctions as moments within an organic unity ; the synthesis is the recognition of each distinction as itself *the whole within which all other distinctions, themselves wholes including it, are included.* No distinction is an ultimate distinction incapable of analysis. Think it as an ultimate distinction, and, behold, in that very thought it becomes a synthetic whole subsuming under it that whole in which you try to consider it as an ultimate element. *In conception, then, subsumption is reciprocal.* The thought-movement,—that is, the dialectic,—by which we go from a distinction within a unity up to that unity, is a movement outwards, which at the same time is not a movement outwards, but a permanent abiding within the point of departure. "Dialectic is the *movement outwards, that remains within,* a movement in which the onesidedness and limitation of the categories of the understanding shows itself to be what in reality it is, namely, its negation." [1] An analysis of a concept as it is in itself, which results in a synthesis of it with a true other ; a synthesis of a concept with its other, which is not an absolutely independent other, but is an other within that concept—this is the dialectical process, this is the dialectical method, which, beginning with a seemingly poor, ultimate, unanalysable concept, reaches the richest concept "without introducing any element from without".[2] "Every new step of the *process outward out of self,* that is, of *further determination,* is also a process within self." [3]

---

[1] *Encyclopædia,* § 81, Werke, vi., 152. Prof. Wallace's translation, "indwelling tendency outwards," of Hegel's "das immanente Ausgehen" not only robs the sentence of its strong paradoxical flavour, but fails to express the vital thought that Hegel expressed in the original.

[2] I., 39 (41).   [3] III., 339 (349).

In closing this examination of Hegel's dialectical method, there are two remarks I wish to make. One of them is that the relation of Hegel's negative to the negative of formal logic is often misstated. It is not true that formal logic deals with a negative that is absolute, with a contradiction that cannot be gainsaid; while speculative logic deals with a negative that is relative, with a contradiction that has no backbone and can be bullied into retractation. The truth is, that the dialectical negative is the only negative that can be thought, and it is an absolute negative. We often make ourselves believe that denial can be a relegation of the denied into another universe than our own, or at least that it can be the expression of the logical non-existence for us of what is denied. And we more often make ourselves believe that contradictions cannot but logically annihilate each other. It is one of Hegel's good offices to philosophy to have pointed out that a negative thought not only *can*, but *must*, be absolute, while no negation can be "bare," and that contradictions are not only thinkable, but that where there is thought, there is contradiction—however, a contradiction *transcended*. The contradictories of formal logic are abstractions, good enough in their own place; but the law of contradiction is not a law of *active* thought; it is merely the law that expresses the relation that exists between two organic elements in thought, when we insist on not regarding their organic character. It is the law that controls the external relation of objects of presentative consciousness, when thought as presented; it is not a law that controls the relation of objects of intellectual consciousness, when thought as intellectual and timeless. In so far as any man thinks, and not merely passively "takes it in," he has transcended the law of contradiction and is under the law of dialectic.

The second remark is, that it follows as a consequence of the *analytic* character of dialectical synthesis, that there is no *external necessity* in the world of thought, in the eternal world that lies behind the world of time and space and is the ground of that temporal and spatial order. In the logical universe, every distinction is itself the whole by virtue of the fact that the other distinctions are logically within it. Every distinction is a monad, a whole logical universe within itself, entirely self-active, knowing no restraint or compulsion from an independent, external source; for everything that is other than it, is an other *in* and *for* it. But that other in and for it is not a *dependent* element in the sense that it for its part looks outside of itself for its ground of being. As it is a logical element, it is likewise itself the whole, in its turn sublating what sublated it.

How many wholes, then, are there ? There is one whole, and there are many wholes; for the hard and fast line of difference that runs between " one " and " many " is a line that can be drawn only when dealing with elements that are thought under the relation of mutual externality. The logical universe can, therefore, with no more propriety be called a monistic universe than a pluralistic one ; nor, on the other hand, is there any more propriety in calling it pluralistic than in calling it monistic, except in the polemical interest of denying an asserted one-sided monism. Neither a pluralism with no real logical unity, nor a monism with no self-active distinctions, is compatible with the laws of thought. And those who read Hegel's monism into a system in which there is no liberty except the one *single* liberty of the one *single* whole, make Hegel do violence to the fundamental law of the totality of each logical distinction, a law which he himself made central within his system. The truth is neither a Spinozism in which the distinctions disappear, nor an idealistic monism [1] in which the distinctions are efficiently operated by a free comprehending unity, not an atheistic pluralism [1] in which there is no logical ground of interrelation between the distinctions. Mere monism and mere pluralism are transcended in the view that emphasises the logical necessity of the free distinctions, and the synthetic as well as analytic character of each of these distinctions. In fine, the truth is neither an absolute *One* at the expense of the Many, nor the separately independent *Many* at the expense of the harmonising unity of the One ; but it is the *unity* of the One and the Many, a logically free One of the logically free Many, which are themselves, each, the One.

And it is just here that logic makes room for ethics. For ethics is possible only when there is interrelation between free self-active centres of consciousness, each recognising itself and others as members of one commonwealth of souls, in which each has rights and duties.[2] Each has rights, be-

---

[1] I do not mean to imply that all idealism is monistic or that all pluralism is atheistic ; all I say is that there is a kind of idealism that is monistic, and a kind of pluralism that is atheistic ; and of both I say that they are logically inadequate.

[2] I wish here to acknowledge my indebtedness to Professor Howison of the University of California for the great help I have received from him on this point,—as indeed on very many others brought out in this series of papers,—although the use I have made of this truth is not such as he would greatly approve, denying as he does any ethical value to Monism.

cause each is the end toward which all work; each has
duties, because each works toward accomplishing the end
of others. Each has rights, because each is the synthetic
unity within which the others function as moments; each
has duties, because each functions as a moment within the
unity of the several others. No logic that does not provide
for such a relation between self-active members of a system
is ethical; no ethics that does not provide an intellectual
and dialectical basis for such a community is logical. And
as the Hegelian ethics rests upon the dialectic, and as the
Hegelian dialectic provides satisfactorily for ethics, the
charge often made that Hegel merely asserts freedom for
the individual without vindicating it, is seen to be baseless.
The Hegelian dialectic is adequate to all scientific needs—
ethical needs among others—because all scientific needs are
but expressions of dialectical necessity; but the Hegelian
dialectic that is adequate, is the *Hegelian* dialectic, not the
pseudo-Hegelian dialectic, which occupies and concerns the
critics. Of course in claiming adequacy for the Hegelian
dialectic I do not claim that it is the last word in philosophy,
or that as Hegel worked it out it is inerrant. All that is
meant is that this insight into the fundamental relation of
the One and the Many is the insight that solves the true
problem of present-day thought, the problem of making an
ethical world intelligible and an intelligible world ethical.